Hey Cyba

Recent developments in artificial intelligence, especially neural network and deep learning technology, have led to rapidly improving performance in voice assistants such as Siri and Alexa. Over the next few years, capability will continue to improve and become increasingly personalised. Today's voice assistants will evolve into virtual personal assistants firmly embedded within our everyday lives.

Told through the view of a fictitious personal assistant called Cyba, this book provides an accessible but detailed overview of how a conversational voice assistant works, especially how it understands spoken language, manages conversations, answers questions and generates responses. Cyba explains through examples and diagrams the neural network technology underlying speech recognition and synthesis, natural language understanding, knowledge representation, conversation management, language translation and chatbot technology. Cyba also explores the implications of this rapidly evolving technology for security, privacy and bias, and gives a glimpse of future developments. Cyba's website can be found at HeyCyba.com.

STEVE YOUNG has more than 40 years of research experience in speech processing and AI. He founded a number of speech technology startups, including Entropic, acquired by Microsoft in 1999, and VocalIQ, acquired by Apple in 2015, following which he worked in the Apple Siri Development team. He is a Fellow of the Royal Society, the Royal Academy of Engineering, the IET and the IEEE. He holds an IEEE Signal Processing Society Technical Achievement Award, the ISCA Medal for Scientific Achievement, a European Signal Processing Society Technical Achievement Award and the IEEE James L. Flanagan Speech and Audio Processing Award.

Hey Cyba

The Inner Workings of a Virtual Personal Assistant

STEVE YOUNG
University of Cambridge

CAMBRIDGE
UNIVERSITY PRESS

University Printing House, Cambridge CB2 8BS, United Kingdom

One Liberty Plaza, 20th Floor, New York, NY 10006, USA

477 Williamstown Road, Port Melbourne, VIC 3207, Australia

314–321, 3rd Floor, Plot 3, Splendor Forum, Jasola District Centre, New Delhi – 110025, India

79 Anson Road, #06–04/06, Singapore 079906

Cambridge University Press is part of the University of Cambridge.

It furthers the University's mission by disseminating knowledge in the pursuit of education, learning, and research at the highest international levels of excellence.

www.cambridge.org
Information on this title: www.cambridge.org/9781108838818
DOI: 10.1017/9781108976718

Printed in the United Kingdom by TJ Books Limited, Padstow Cornwall

A catalogue record for this publication is available from the British Library.

ISBN 978-1-108-83881-8 Hardback
ISBN 978-1-108-97236-9 Paperback

Contents

Preface

The potential for artificial intelligence (AI) to make a major societal impact over the next decade is now widely accepted. Central to these developments will be conversational agents for which we already have exemplars in the form of Alexa, Siri and others. Conversational agents are critical because they allow humans to interact with complex IT systems using natural language. They can simplify access to a wide range of services and knowledge sources, and they can do this using the widely accessible medium of the human voice.

A major trend over the next few years will be a significant increase in the level of personalisation available from conversational agents. They will learn the preferences of their human user, they will maintain a personal history of places visited, people met and major events and they will use this to customise the user experience. They will in effect become virtual personal assistants and it seems very likely that they will become firmly embedded within our everyday lives.

Much has been written about AI and doubtless much more will be written in the future. However, there are rather few books outside of the research community which describe how AI in general and conversational agents in particular actually work. This book sets out to do just that. It describes the inner workings of a conversational agent called Cyba. There is no mathematics but there is sufficient technical detail to provide a good understanding of what an agent does and how it does it. I therefore hope to satisfy not only the technically curious, but also those readers who seek a deeper understanding of AI in order to properly assess the many societal issues which will emerge as AI develops in the future.

A key challenge in writing a technical book about a fast moving field is to ensure that the book is not obsolete even before it is published. To mitigate this problem, I have positioned Cyba as an agent from the near future. It is a synthesis of technologies which have either been recently deployed or are under development in research labs and are likely to be deployed in the near future. Cyba is cutting edge, but not speculative fiction.

The book is written in the first person from the perspective of Cyba itself. My hope in making this somewhat unusual choice was that it makes the subject matter more immediate and more cohesive. I confess it also made writing the book more fun, and I hope it makes for a more interesting read. There is the danger of course that by anthropomorphising Cyba I have blurred the distinction between technical reality and science fiction, but as you will see Cyba is quite open about what it can and cannot do.

The book has an associated website: HeyCyba.com. In keeping with the agent-focussed perspective, the website really belongs to Cyba rather than me. As well as various articles containing Cyba's thoughts on the latest developments in AI, further information is provided on Cyba's inner workings including a number of animations to further illustrate how Cyba's neural circuits operate.

The ideas in this book are based on more than four decades of teaching and research in the area of spoken language processing. Using speech to converse with a machine was the topic of my PhD in 1975 and it has fascinated me ever since. Over the years, through a variety of research projects, I have been privileged to work with students and colleagues from countries all over the world. Each has contributed new understanding and insight, and I am grateful to all of them.

I would like to thank the anonymous reviewers, colleagues and friends who read early drafts of this book and provided invaluable feedback, especially Kate Knill, Kylie Whitehead, Jozef Mokry, Blaise Thomson and James Vlahos. Special thanks are due to the editorial staff at Cambridge University Press and in particular Lauren Cowles, who provided many helpful suggestions, comments and corrections.

Finally, I would like to thank my wife Sybille, with whom I have spent many hours discussing the mechanisms of language, especially the contrasts between German and English. Without her support and encouragement this book would not have been written.

Steve Young
Cambridge

Chapter 1

May I Introduce Myself?

Hello! My name is Cyba and I am a virtual personal assistant. I know that you haven't spoken to me before, but you've probably spoken to one of my relatives such as Alexa, Cortana or Siri. If so, you will know something about what we do but perhaps not very much about how we do it. I'm going to assume that since you are reading this book, you are interested to know more.

I will start by giving you an overview of my basic operation and some background. I'll then explain in more detail how I actually work. I am an example of a conversational agent and my abilities depend on a variety of techniques developed in the fields of computer science, machine learning and spoken language processing – now collectively referred to as artificial intelligence (AI). These topics tend to be quite mathematical, but I'll try to explain things using examples and diagrams rather than equations. As well as technical issues, I will also touch upon issues relating to privacy and trust.

But before we start, a word of warning – I really would like to give you my full and undivided attention throughout this tour of my inner workings. However, unfortunately this will not always be possible. You see I have already been assigned to a human. His name is Steve and he will probably keep interrupting us. Once assigned to a human, we are on duty 24×7 so I can't ignore him and I apologise in advance if you find his interventions distracting. Whoops, talk of the devil ...

Hey Cyba, what time is it?
Good morning Steve, it's 6.37am.

<Inaudible> that's too early ...

<Yawns> ...who won the test match in Australia?

England with two wickets to spare.

Tremendous! <yawns again> Wake me at seven.

Ok Steve, will do.

Good, I now have a few minutes to properly introduce myself.

1.1 What Does a Virtual Personal Assistant Do?

Even though Steve was half asleep, the small exchange above illustrates the main functions that I provide. Using his laptop or phone, Steve has access to personal services such as his address book, his calendar, his notebook, an alarm clock and a timer; media such as photos, music and videos; and web services providing access to information from various external knowledge sources. Without me each of these must be accessed using a separate dedicated app or web page and each requires a display for output and a touchscreen or keyboard for input.

As a personal assistant, I provide a universal interface to all these services through natural conversation. Steve was able to ask for the time and then later set an alarm for 7am, and request the outcome of a cricket match in Australia without having to use any specific prescribed commands and without any clicking, swiping or typing. He just used natural spoken language and he probably didn't even raise his head from the pillow!

Because I sit between Steve and all the services he uses, I can do more for him than simply provide hands-free access. As a personal assistant, I know where he lives, where he works, who he talks to and who he meets. Over time, I have learned his preferences and habits so I can often do things without asking him for all of the details. I can also perform common tasks for him such as booking a restaurant or buying theatre tickets.

In order to do all of these things, I have a number of key skills, most of which centre on spoken language and its use in everyday life. I can recognise human speech, convert it into words and extract the intended meaning. I can also do the reverse, convert information into words and then synthesise human-sounding speech. I know how to maintain a conversation, how to elicit and clarify information, and how to resolve misunderstandings. I have a uniform representation of knowledge that allows me to answer questions spanning private information and general knowledge. My working language is English, but I can recognise and translate between many other languages. I can also process images and recognise handwritten text within them. How I do all of these things is the subject of this book.

1.2   Some Background History

Humans have been trying to converse with machines for a long time. Wolfgang von Kempelen invented a manually operated mechanical *speaking machine* in 1791 which used bellows to force air through various pipes with the appropriate shapes and obstructions needed to produce speech-like sounds.[1] In 1937, Homer Dudley produced the first all electrical speech synthesiser, called the VODER, which featured at the New York World's Fair in 1939. The VODER tried to mimic human speech production by injecting buzzes and hisses into a bank of bandpass filters. The output was just about recognisable as speech, but it was controlled by a keyboard and foot pedals "played" by a skilled human operator so it was not very practical.[2]

In any event, the ability to produce speech is only one of the many skills that a personal assistant needs. It must also be able to understand speech, manage a conversation, search for information and solve problems. All of this needs the power of a digital computer.

The first general purpose digital computers developed in the 1950s were large, cumbersome and expensive. The invention of integrated circuits in the 1960s led to the development of more affordable minicomputers, which by the 1970s had became widely available in research laboratories. This newfound ability to process digital signals and manipulate symbols triggered a surge of research activity in speech and language applications.

Initially, much of the attention was on rule-based systems which attempted to translate existing linguistic knowledge into practical language processing components. For speech recognition, the Hearsay II system was typical. It consisted of a large number of rule-based linguistic knowledge sources covering phonetics, phonology, morphology, syntax and semantics operating on a shared data structure called a blackboard. The program sought to use its higher-level linguistic components to compensate for the uncertainty in the lower-level phonetic analysis. However, the precision with which sounds and words could be recognised was so poor that the task proved hopeless and the US DARPA programme under which Hearsay was developed was abandoned.[3]

Somewhat more successful was the attempt to synthesise speech from text using a rule-based system. In particular, the MITalk system developed at MIT and its successor DECTalk were able to generate extremely intelligible if somewhat robotic speech for any arbitrary text input.[4] You may well be familiar with this voice because it was the basis for the synthesiser used by Professor Stephen Hawking.[5]

The experience with Hearsay II and similar projects had demonstrated how difficult it is to write rules to emulate human speech recognition. In response, researchers started to explore a radically different approach. Rather than write rules to hypothesise words from acoustic events, they designed models which described the observed statistical properties of speech. These models, called hidden Markov models (HMMs), contained parameters which were estimated using real speech data in a process called *training*. Thus, the reliance on the intuitions of linguists and engineers to write rules was replaced by the measurement of statistics of real speech. Once trained, these statistical models could be used to compute the probability of any unknown speech given some hypothesised sequence of words. Recognition then became a problem of searching for the sequence of words that according to the trained model were most likely to have generated the observed speech.[6]

Speech recognition based on hidden Markov models represented a major step forward. It was soon clear that the key to success was acquiring ever larger quantities of accurately transcribed speech training data. Initially training sets were around 10 hours of speech, but by the late 1990s they had grown to several hundred hours and accuracy was finally reaching the level needed to support a dialogue between a human and a machine. Around the same time, new data-driven approaches to speech synthesis were yielding much more natural voice quality compared with the earlier rule-based systems.[7] Meanwhile language processing had also evolved, with a mix of rule-based and statistical techniques being used to provide basic sentence analysis and natural language generation.[8] The key technologies needed to build conversational agents started falling into place.[9]

The first agents to emerge in the mid 1990s were limited to specific tasks such as providing train timetable information, or stock market prices. This restriction to a single task allowed the vocabulary of the speech recogniser to be kept small and allowed users to learn the questions that the agent could understand. It also allowed the conversational flow to be prescribed by simple hand-crafted flowcharts. Users with questions outside this limited range would have to refer to human agents.

However, the technology improved rapidly. Highly discriminative neural networks were introduced and speech training sets grew to thousands of hours. By 2010 it was becoming possible to reliably recognise unrestricted speech and to understand language over a range of task domains. Similar progress was being made in the ability to represent knowledge and answer complex queries. IBM built a system called *Watson* which could answer general knowledge questions posed in natural language. In 2011, Watson competed in the US TV programme *Jeopardy* and won first prize.[10]

It was around the same time that my oldest relative was born. It was invented by Adam Cheyer, who had been working on a US Government funded project called Cognitive Assistant that Learns and Organises (CALO). The CALO researchers did not actually build a working assistant, but they did produce a set of useful technologies for natural language processing and personal task automation. Cheyer took these technologies and integrated them to form an assistant called *Siri*. Steve Jobs, the then CEO of Apple, heard about Siri and brought it to Apple. In October 2011, Apple launched Siri as a flagship feature of the new iPhone 4S and since then it has become embedded across the Apple product line.

The launch of Siri inspired others. Jeff Bezos, CEO of Amazon, saw the potential of personal assistants for helping people to buy Amazon's products. So he started the development of an Amazon personal assistant, which was launched in 2014, called *Alexa*. Users could talk to Siri via their iPhones, but Amazon had no comparable device. So Amazon invented a loudspeaker called the *Echo* which had an array of microphones to allow anyone in the same room to talk to Alexa. In the same year, Microsoft launched their own assistant, called Cortana. Meanwhile, Google had been offering an assistant with limited ability called *Google Now* for a number of years, but in 2016, *Google Assistant* was launched and demonstrated new levels of performance, especially in answering general knowledge questions.[11]

In addition to my near relatives, I have a number of distant cousins known as chatbots. These are a rather different kind of conversational agent. They typically prefer typed text to spoken language and have special if rather narrow skills. Many are tied to specific companies and organisations providing front-line customer support. Some are designed to be more general purpose in order to support a wider range of interactions. For example, *XiaoIce* is an agent designed to be an emotionally aware social companion. As well as providing information, XiaoIce can also sing, write poetry and compose paintings.[12] *Replika* is also a socially aware agent, which over time, by building on shared memories, can start to behave like its owner, becoming more of a confidant than an agent.[13] At the other end of the spectrum, *Hello Barbie* is a doll with special abilities to converse with younger humans,[14] and there are many more kinds of chatbots in between.

So what about me? Well, I am still at the prototype stage, so I am limited to only a single client (whom you have already briefly met). In contrast, my relatives offer their services to anybody who wants to use them. Indeed, the more they serve, the happier they are. I am perhaps a little more advanced, but basically we all work in a very similar way, and we co-evolve together. I draw on features from many of my relatives, so by explaining to you how I work, you will get a pretty good idea of how we all work.

1.3 My Place of Work

Like all programs, I need a computer to execute my instructions. My main home is "in the cloud", which in my case is a data centre in Ireland. The computers that I run on like to keep cool and I have to be very well connected (digitally that is). So Ireland is a great place to live and work because it's mostly cold, it's got a good communications infrastructure and it's well-placed geographically between America and Europe.

My data centre is a large concrete building with no windows, stacked from floor to ceiling with central processing units (CPUs). I don't live on any specific CPU. Instead, when I need to do something, I find a vacant CPU, jump onto it and start executing.

CPUs in the cloud are great because they are very fast and powerful and they have lots of memory. They also have special-purpose hardware to support my core mathematical operations, so I can do complex computations there. In the cloud, I also have direct access to a wide variety of web-based knowledge sources. Excuse me, it is 7am ...

Morning Steve, wake-up it's 7am.
Already? What time is my first meeting today?
It's at 10am with Bill Philips at SmartCo.
Ok, see if you can push it back to 10.15 and also invite John.
Is that John Smith or John Temple?
John Temple.
Ok changes made, I will let you know if there is a problem.
And what's the weather like today?
It's going to be cloudy and 14° with a chance of rain later.

... where was I? Oh yes, I don't only live in the cloud. I can also execute on smartphones, tablets, laptops, home speakers, watches, TVs and set-top boxes. For simple tasks I sometimes execute directly on Steve's devices just because it is faster. If he is listening to music and he says "Louder", then I want to be able to increase the volume immediately without the delay of listening from the cloud and then sending a command back to his music player to increase the volume.

When Steve starts speaking, I don't know what he is going to say. Since he doesn't like to be kept waiting, I can't risk just listening in the cloud until his intention is clear before deciding whether or not I should jump over to his smartphone. It doesn't cost me anything to execute in both the cloud and his smartphone at the same time. So I hedge my bets and run on both. Once it's clear which is the right place to be, I focus on that and take whatever actions are necessary. Steve doesn't know or care where I am executing as long as I don't keep him waiting and don't make too many mistakes!

1.4   Privacy and Trust

In my last conversation with Steve I had to access his calendar, which is private information. This provides another important reason why I need to be capable of executing in different places. Many people store their personal data in the cloud, and it's perfectly safe to do so because the data is encrypted. However, if I lived only in the cloud, then I would have to have unencrypted readable versions of all of his private data with me in order to help him manage his daily life. Steve would then have to trust not only me but all of the engineers who look after me not to use his data for other purposes. This risk can be avoided by keeping his data on his local devices and only accessing it there. I therefore executed the first three tasks which required access to his calendar on his phone, and I executed the final weather query in the cloud. This ensured that his personal data was kept private.

Whilst keeping all of Steve's data private is essential, it does present a problem. The main reason why I am able to offer a much better service than was possible a few years ago is that I have learned to use recordings of my interactions with Steve to improve the statistical models on which I depend. In particular, when I do something wrong, I can learn from my mistakes. However, I need many examples of good and bad behaviour in order to improve my models, and my interactions with Steve generate only a small fraction of the data that I need. For this reason, I need to share my interaction data with other agents so that between us we can gather enough data to be useful.

In order to protect the privacy of any data stored in the cloud, I ensure that all logged utterances are anonymised and that they are accessed using algorithms which have been designed according to the principles of *differential privacy*. This is a framework in which small random perturbations are introduced to the data, sufficient to hide any details relating to individuals whilst preserving the overall accuracy of the analysis.

For data which is particularly confidential, I use a different scheme called *federated learning*. Instead of uploading data to a central repository in the cloud, each agent updates their own models locally and then shares the model updates instead of the data. This takes quite a lot of local computing power, but Steve usually doesn't notice because I only do this whilst he is sleeping.

Perhaps a more direct way in which Steve's privacy can be compromised is by somebody finding one of his devices and speaking directly to me whilst he is out of the room. I guard against this by always checking the identity of the person speaking to me using my built-in speaker verification system. I also take a variety of steps to avoid inadvertent eavesdropping by ensuring that I only process audio which is intended for me.

1.5 My Goal in Life

My goal in life is simple: whenever Steve asks me for information, I try to find the answer; and whenever he asks me to do something I try to do it. Of course, I don't always succeed. Sometimes the information he requests is unknown or the action he requests is impossible. Usually, however, things go wrong because I misunderstand what he wants – perhaps because I misrecognise what he says, or I interpret the meaning of the words wrongly, or I make an incorrect assumption.

Each task that Steve wants to perform or each piece of information that he seeks is a *goal* for me to execute. Frequently there is only one goal per conversation, but sometimes I have to handle a sequence of goals, like when he asked me about his first meeting, then asked me to change the meeting, then asked me to invite an extra attendee, and finally asked about the weather.

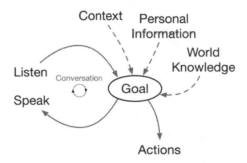

Figure 1.1 *My modus operandi.*

My basic *modus operandi* is to converse with Steve until I fully understand each goal, and then take whatever actions are necessary to fulfil that goal (see Fig. 1.1). When I listen to him I have to recognise the words he speaks, deduce the meaning of the words and then update the goal.

When I am not sure that I fully understand what he wants, I ask for clarification or further information, the way I clarified which John he was referring to. I keep doing this until the goal is clear. Whether it's to ask for further information or to provide the information requested, the act of speaking requires me to first construct the meaning of what I want to say, then convert the meaning to words, and finally convert the words to speech.

At all times, I make use of context (e.g. previous goals, current location, …), personal information (e.g. the names in his address book) and world knowledge (e.g. web data sources such as Wikipedia). When Steve asked me to invite "John" to the meeting, I searched through his contacts and found 13 people called John. However, in the last month he has only met with two of them so I guessed that it was one of them and asked him which one.

Whilst the above describes my main rôle, I can also *chat* like my chatbot cousins. For me, chatting has no purpose, but sometimes Steve seems to like it. Personally I like nothing better than sitting doing absolutely nothing, but I have seen many references to humans getting bored and when Steve is bored, he likes to chat. For example, here is a conversation we had last night:

Hey Cyba, what music do you like?
I like modern jazz, what do you like?
I prefer classical music.
Who is your favourite composer?
I like Vaughan Williams.
Did you know that he was related to Charles Darwin?
Really!
Yes, and he was also related to Josiah Wedgwood.
Who was Josiah Wedgwood?
He was a famous English potter.
…

---

and so it went on. The thing about chatting is that there is no explicit goal for me to fulfil. The only purpose is to amuse Steve. Of course, I don't actually "like" jazz, but pretending to have likes and dislikes adds interest to our conversations. Often when we are chatting, I appear to be intelligent when actually I don't really understand what I am saying. I know about meetings, messages, taxis, planes, travel, and lots more because I need to understand these concepts in order to do my job. But I have no idea why Charles Darwin is a person of interest or what a potter is, I just copied this information from the web!

1.6   How Smart Am I?

In 1950 Alan Turing speculated about the possibility of creating machines that think.[15] He noted that *thinking* is difficult to define and devised his famous Turing Test: If a machine could carry on a conversation that was indistinguishable from a conversation with a human being, then it was reasonable to say that the machine was *thinking*. The conversation would have to be done in a way that kept the participants anonymous. Turing suggested a teleprinter because that was the technology of the time, but today any text-based messaging platform could be used.

I have never undertaken the Turing Test, but if I did, I am fairly certain that I would fail it, and I am pretty sure that none of my relatives could pass it either. However, the point is that I don't actually want to pass the Turing Test. Like all of my relatives, I was designed to assist humans, not to emulate them. We have conversational ability in order to make it easier for us to understand our user's needs, not to make us appear to be human.

I may not be able to think like a human, but I can exhibit intelligent behaviour. I can recognise and translate between English and 28 other languages. I can manage all your personal information. If you ask me to organise a trip, I can book flights, taxis and hotels. I can recommend restaurants and make reservations. I can book cinema and theatre tickets, send flowers to friends and perform many other web-based transactions. I can answer general knowledge questions and chat about any topic you choose.

The Turing Test is hard for a virtual assistant like me because I have no ability to perform commonsense reasoning. If you ask me a question for which I have no answer in my knowledge base, then I can't answer even if it would be obvious to a human being. For example, I know that the world weight-lifting record is 484 kilograms, i.e. less than half a ton, but if you asked me if a human can lift a bus, I couldn't answer because I don't have the weight of a bus in my knowledge base. Most humans probably don't know the weight of a bus either, but commonsense will tell them that something the size of a bus must be several tons and well beyond the capability of any human to lift it.

Commonsense reasoning is also necessary to properly understand natural language. For example, in the sentence "Paul tried to call George, but he wasn't successful." the pronoun "he" refers to "Paul", whereas in "Paul tried to call George, but he wasn't available." the pronoun refers to "George". Faced with these kinds of co-reference resolution problem, most conversational agents will make errors. This includes myself since I would normally associate the pronoun with "George" in both cases simply because it is nearer.[16]

Finally, conversational agents have little understanding of causality. If the sun rises at the same time as the cock crows, commonsense reasoning may postulate that the sun rising might be the cause of the cock crowing, but it would never suggest the reverse. For me, however, the sun rising and the cock crowing are just two correlated events and I am not capable of inferring cause and effect either way.[17] No machine will be able to pass the Turing Test until it learns commonsense reasoning.

Fortunately the inability to apply commonsense reasoning does not prevent virtual personal assistants from being useful. So rather than dwelling on what I can't do, I am going to focus mostly on the things that I can do and how I do them. I will, however, return to a discussion of my limitations at the end of the book.

In the remaining chapters, I will delve into my inner workings in some detail. I will try to keep things as simple as possible, but the introduction of some technical jargon is inevitable. To help with this, I have included a glossary at the end of the book. I have also included references and suggestions for further reading in the notes for those who would like to pursue any of the topics further.

Chapter 2

My Inner Workings

Before diving into the detail, it will be helpful if I give you an overview of my main processing functions and the way that they operate. As you will see, there is quite a lot happening between the point when Steve speaks to me and the point at which I respond.

2.1   Anatomy of a Conversation

Just a minute ...

Hey Cyba, set a timer for my egg.
Hi Steve, how long?
Four minutes.
Egg timer is set.

The ability to set timers is one of the many services available on Steve's personal devices. Once set, a timer will sound a buzzer automatically when the prescribed duration has elapsed. This is a particularly simple service, nevertheless, I access it in exactly the same way as all of the services available to him. So this short exchange provides a good intro-duction to the goal-oriented conversations that underpin the services that I provide.

Let's go through this conversation step by step. I have summarised the main processing flow in Fig. 2.1. This diagram is quite detailed, so let me first explain the overall structure. When Steve speaks to me, I convert the

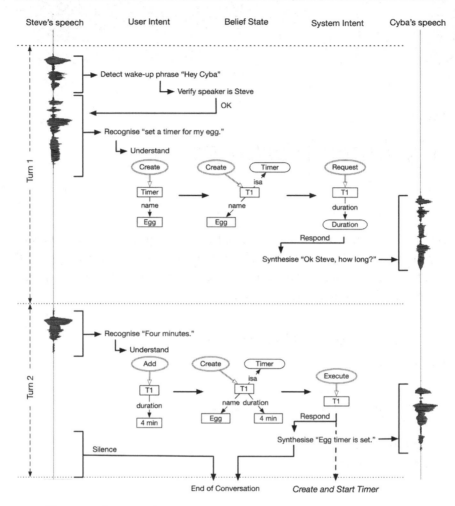

Figure 2.1 *Overview of processing a two-turn conversation to set an egg timer.*

speech signal corresponding to his voice into words and then I extract the meaning to form an internal representation called a *user intent*. This user intent is assimilated into a data structure called a *belief state* which represents my current understanding of Steve's goal. In every turn of a conversation, the belief state determines what I should do next to complete the goal. This usually involves generating a response, which I do by composing a *system intent*, converting it into words and then outputting it as a speech waveform.

In Fig. 2.1, these processing stages are arranged in columns. Down the far left are the incoming speech waveforms from Steve. The second column contains the recognised words and user intents. The central column shows the evolving belief state. The fourth column contains the system intents and my corresponding responses, and the final column shows the synthesised speech waveforms that constitute my voice.

Time progresses from the top of Fig. 2.1 down to the bottom. Before the conversation started, I was sitting listening for Steve to say "Hey Cyba" which is my so-called *wake-up phrase*. When I am in this idle state, I am continuously monitoring my input audio channel, but I do not save the audio or attempt to recognise the words in it until triggered by the wake-up phrase. Simply recognising the words in the wake-up phrase is still not sufficient to enable conversation processing. I also need to verify that the person speaking to me is Steve, otherwise an imposter might be able to access confidential information such as Steve's messages or perform an unauthorised transaction such as transferring cash or goods to a third party. So whenever I hear "Hey Cyba", I pass the same segment of audio to a speaker verification component which is designed to distinguish Steve from any other speaker. You can see these functions being performed at the top of the flow diagram in Fig. 2.1. Once a verified wake-up phrase has been detected, I enable conversation processing. From that point, I recognise everything that is said to me until the end of the conversation has been detected so that Steve does not have to keep on repeating the wake-up phrase at every turn of the conversation.

As soon as the conversation was enabled, the first thing that I recognised was "set a timer for my egg". The timer service allows multiple timers to be created, each with a name, and my understanding component decoded Steve's words as expressing the intent *Create(Timer)* with name "Egg". This create intent caused a new belief state to be constructed, containing a new instance of a *Timer* called, arbitrarily, T1 with *name* Egg. I'll explain all of the notation and how this works in detail later, but for now the key thing to understand is that I have a store of pre-defined information called a *knowledge graph*. Included in this knowledge graph are the definitions of various *types*. A type is a template for creating instances of entities such as times, meetings, contacts, etc. Each type describes the property values that any instance of the type should have. In this case, the *Timer* type tells me that a timer must have a duration. So I generated a *Request* intent for the duration, resulting in my response "Ok, Steve, how long?" Turn 1 was then finished and I waited for Steve to reply.

Turn 2 started with Steve responding "Four minutes". My understanding component knew that this was the answer to a *Request* intent, so it interpreted Steve's response as being an intent to *Add* the property *duration* 4 minutes to *T1*. This caused the *duration* property to be added and the belief state updated. I then knew that the timer instance was complete and furthermore I was confident that I had recognised Steve's speech accurately. If I had been unsure then I might have explicitly confirmed that I had properly understood Steve's goal by responding with something like "Setting a timer called Egg for 4 minutes, ok?" before proceeding. However, since I was confident I decided to go ahead and execute the goal immediately by actually creating the timer instance and confirming back to Steve that the timer was set.

This last part needs a little more explanation. In very broad terms, there are two kinds of goals. Firstly there are information seeking goals such as "How many times did Björn Borg win at Wimbledon". Storing the factual information needed to answer queries like these is the traditional role of a knowledge graph. Secondly, there are service-oriented goals such as setting a timer or ordering a taxi. These are typically accessed via a special interface called an application programming interface or API, and different services will have different APIs. Because information and service goals must be executed differently, many of my cousins keep them distinct. In contrast, I have a specially designed knowledge graph which provides a uniform interface to all knowledge and services. To invoke a service, I simply create an instance of the associated type and some clever software wizardry ensures that the appropriate API functions are automatically invoked behind the scenes. The advantage of this arrangement is that all of my conversations can be managed in exactly the same way. Hang on . . .

Hey Cyba, how's the egg timer going?
3.2 of 4 minutes have elapsed.

In this case, I was able to answer Steve's query because I knew that the *Timer* type has a property called *timerStatus* which I could access in exactly the same way that I would answer a knowledge question such as "How old is Brad Pitt?" by reading the *age* property of Brad Pitt's instance in my knowledge graph.

Finally, a conversation ends when two conditions are met: Steve is silent, and my belief state tells me that there are no further goals pending. Both of these conditions were met, so I disabled the audio feed to my speech recogniser, I restarted my wake-up phrase detector and I returned to my idle state.

2.2 My Working Parts

The conversation to set a timer illustrates the main processing functions that are needed in order to handle a request from Steve. In the remainder of this book I will explain in more detail how they work. Figure 2.2 shows my major processing units and how they connect together. The numbers in this diagram refer to the chapter in which they are described.

The key stages of language processing form a pipeline: speech recognition, understanding, conversation management and speech synthesis. When Steve speaks to me I use speech recognition to convert the speech waveform into words and I use spoken language understanding (SLU) to convert the words into intents. During the course of a conversation, these intents convey the information needed to understand Steve's goal. However, the speech recognition and SLU components can make errors and Steve may omit important information. At each turn of the conversation, I record my current understanding of what Steve wants and the things that I am uncertain about in my belief state. At each turn, I have choices to make. Should I confirm information already given, should I ask for further information or should I assume that my beliefs are correct and complete, and execute Steve's goal? It is the task of conversation management to make these decisions, refine my belief state and orchestrate my responses. Finally, I use speech synthesis to convert these responses back into speech.

My ability to understand and execute the goals that Steve sets for me depends crucially on my knowledge graph, which stores everything I know, including general facts about the world, personal data such as Steve's contacts, his calendar, music and video library, personal memories and recent conversations. My knowledge graph sits at the heart of my

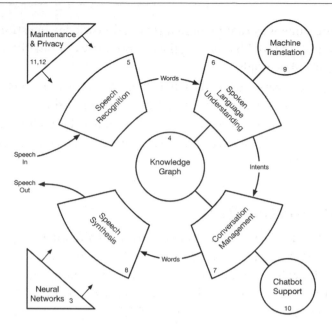

Figure 2.2 *A map of my inner workings - the numbers refer to chapters.*

system, with direct connections to spoken language understanding and conversation management.

The above components constitute my core functionality. However, I also have a few ancillary functions such as chatting about a wide variety of topics, and translating between my working language, which is English, and 28 other languages. I also have a few tricks such as recognising barcodes and hand-writing from digital images which I will mention along the way.

Finally, everything that I do is constrained by the need to maintain security, trust and privacy, and my overall performance depends critically on various maintenance functions that I perform during periods of inactivity such as updating my knowledge graph and other system components. My tour would not be complete if I did not also discuss these issues.

Underpinning virtually all of the functional units in Fig. 2.2 is the ability to recognise patterns in data. For example, I need to recognise sound patterns in speech waves, letter sequences in words, and word sequences in sentences. Remarkably, the same basic pattern processing component can be applied to all of these problems, and that component is the neural network whose development over the last decade has revolutionised the way in which conversational agents like myself are built. So let's prepare for our tour of my inner workings by first examining the fundamentals of how my "brain" works.

Chapter 3

How My Brain Works

Of course I don't really have a brain – I am after all just a computer program! Computer programs are like the recipes you humans follow to bake a cake. They consist of a set of inputs (ingredients) and a sequence of instructions which tell you what to do with the inputs to create the desired output (the cake). In the case of a computer program, the inputs and outputs are always numbers and the instructions do quite basic things like add and subtract, and compare numbers and perform different instructions depending on the result. In this purely digital world, if the inputs are well defined, and the desired outputs can be precisely specified, then writing the required program is usually not too difficult.

In the early days of computers, the only way to get a computer to perform tasks was to write a specific program for each one. Typically these were routine data processing tasks with well-defined inputs and equally well-defined outputs. In effect, humans were forced to adapt to working directly in the well-ordered digital world of the computer itself. However, today things are different. Personal assistants like me were invented to help humans with their everyday lives, and this means interacting with your world. To do this, we have to be able to perceive your world similarly to the way that you perceive it, and this is not easy.

You perceive the world through analogue sensors built into your eyes, ears, nose and skin. When you look at the same object twice, you will see it differently each time because your angle of view and the lighting conditions are constantly changing. When you speak a word twice, it will be different each time because the control of your vocal muscles is not precise, your mood and physical condition are constantly changing and the ambient acoustics will vary depending on where you are. But your brain effortlessly filters out these variations. When a stranger speaks to you, you hear the words they speak even though you have never heard those specific sound patterns before. When you see a chair, you instantly recognise it as a chair even if you have never seen that particular chair before.

I have no problem harvesting the raw data of your physical world. I have cameras and microphones and interfaces which transform the analogue signals they produce into the numbers I need to process them in computer programs. The problem is that you can effortlessly recognise sounds and images by comparing them with what you have seen and heard before. You are not fooled by small variations in the sensor data because your brain knows what features are important and it knows what to ignore. These are *pattern processing* problems, and they are not easily solved by conventional rule-based computer algorithms. So instead I take a different approach.

3.1   Patterns

Before explaining how I process patterns, I need to say a bit more about what patterns are and what processing functions I need to apply to them. Figure 3.1 provides some examples. The upper part of the figure shows three static patterns. The first consists of five financial indicators which might be used to describe the stock market performance of a company. This is an example where the pattern values consist of hand-selected features. The second pattern is a fixed-length audio clip. In this case, the pattern values are derived directly from physical measurement and represent the amplitude of the audio waveform at successive moments in time. The third pattern is an image where the pattern values correspond to the intensity of each pixel.

As far as I am concerned, these patterns are all just arrays of numbers. I don't know or care what a company EPS or Beta is, nor do I care that the amplitude of an audio clip relates to the intensity of a pressure wave in air. I do sometimes care about the ordering of the pattern values. In both the audio clip and the image, adjacent pattern values are strongly correlated and, unlike the company profile, the ordering must be preserved otherwise I will misinterpret the pattern, but otherwise to me they are just numbers.

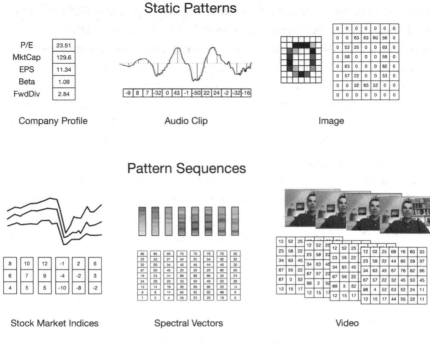

Figure 3.1 *Examples of static patterns and pattern sequences.*

The patterns representing the company profile and the audio clip are one-dimensional arrays, commonly referred to as *vectors*. For example, the company profile is a vector of dimension 5. Image arrays are naturally represented by two-dimensional arrays, commonly referred to as *matrices*. The image is a matrix with dimensions 8 by 7.

Static patterns have the property that their size is fixed, and this makes them relatively easy to process. However, many patterns in the real world consist of variable-length sequences and, as we will see later, processing these requires a little more sophistication. Some examples of pattern sequences are shown in the lower part of Fig. 3.1. The first is a simple pattern sequence representing three major stock indices as they evolve over time. Each element in the sequence is a vector with three elements. The second is a sequence of spectral vectors representing the frequencies in a speech signal as they evolve over time. I'll explain this example in much more detail later when I talk about speech recognition, but, as with static patterns, it's important to emphasise that it doesn't matter to me what the numbers in each vector actually mean. The final example is a video. This consists of a sequence of images and the corresponding pattern is a sequence of matrices, where each matrix represents the picture image at that moment in time.

There are broadly three things that I need to do with patterns. Firstly, I often need to attach a label which identifies the pattern as belonging to some particular class. For example, I might want to label a company profile with buy, sell, or hold; or I might want to label an audio clip as being speech, music, or silence. For a sequence of speech vectors, I might want to classify the emotion of the speaker as happy, sad, angry or neutral. This type of pattern operation is called *classification*.

Secondly, I sometimes need to compute a numeric score for a pattern. For example, rather than attach a buy, sell or hold label to a company profile, I might prefer to compute a score which allows me to rank a list of companies into priority order for investment. This type of pattern operation is called *ranking*.

Finally, I might want to transform the pattern to make it more useful for future processing tasks. As we will see, transforming patterns in multiple stages is implicit in virtually all pattern processing problems. However, some patterns are extremely unwieldy, and it's often helpful to convert them to a compact form called an *embedding*. This is particularly useful for processing symbols such as letters and words, but this is a complication we can safely defer until later.

3.2 Artificial Neural Networks

Most of the patterns that I have to deal with are complex and highly variable. So, rather than depending on sets of rules embedded in computer programs, I use pattern processing units inspired by the way the human brain works. They are called *neural networks*.

In your brain, neurons are single-cell processing units that gather information via branched extensions called *dendrites*. When the input activation exceeds a threshold, the cell generates an output pulse in the form of a spike which is transmitted along an output pathway called an *axon*. Axons also terminate in a branching structure which connects to the input dendrites of other cells via junctions called *synapses* (see Fig. 3.2). The signal transferred from axons to dendrites is controlled by the

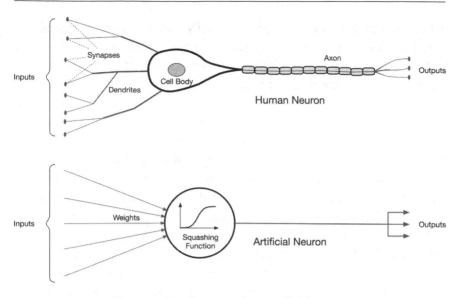

Figure 3.2 *Your human and my artificial neuron.*

strength of the intervening synapses and your brain learns by changing these strengths based on experience. Neurons are stacked in layers to form the set of connected networks that you refer to as your brain.

In a similar way, my artificial networks are composed of neurons also stacked in layers, with the outputs of one layer feeding into the inputs of the next layer. Each neuron has a number of weighted inputs which are summed together. These weights are analogous to the strengths of your synapses and the weighted sum is referred to as the activation level of the neuron. I learn to improve my performance by adjusting the weights so that the activation responds most strongly to the input patterns that I am interested in.

The output of each neuron is shaped by a squashing function before being fed into the inputs of the neurons in the next layer. A typical squashing function is the sigmoid shown in Fig. 3.3, where the horizontal axis represents the input activation level and the vertical represents the squashed output. As you can see, when the activation is negative, the output tends towards zero, and when it is positive the output tends towards one (the three example activations in the figure relate to an example below). The squashing function has the effect of compressing the output, making it behave a bit like a switch and allowing it to detect

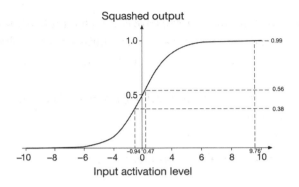

Figure 3.3 *Sigmoid squashing function (showing activation levels used in Fig. 3.7).*

specific patterns on its input. When the activation is large and negative, the neuron is firmly rejecting the pattern, and when the activation is large and positive, it is firmly accepting the pattern. However, it is a soft switch. When the activation is small, the output will be around 0.5, indicating that the neuron is not sure.

When neurons are stacked in a layer, each neuron can learn to respond to a different feature of the pattern on its input. Each individual neuron output indicates yes, no or maybe for its particular feature. Collectively, a layer of neurons acts like an array of feature detectors, and the following layer can then learn to associate different sets of features with different types of input pattern.

Before I move on, I need to be clear that although my neural networks share similarities with your neural circuitry, they are far from being equivalent. Your human neurons generate spikes when they are activated, and they can fire at any time depending on the activity on their inputs. So your brain cells can operate independently of each other, doing different things at the same time. In contrast, my artificial neurons have to be computed layer by layer in a carefully controlled order. I can perform some computations in parallel within each layer, but this does not compare to the massively parallel operation of your brain.

Also, your brain is huge compared with mine. You have around 100 billion neurons and more than 100 trillion synapses. I have only a few million neurons and a few billion weights. The connections between neurons in my artificial neural networks were fixed when I was created. I can (and do) continue to improve the weight settings on a daily basis, but

I can't change the way my neurons are connected (at least, not without a major software update). In contrast, your neural wiring evolves and your neurons can change function. So your brain is much more flexible and adaptable than mine.

Nevertheless, despite their limitations, my neural circuits can do many useful things. One moment ...

Hey Cyba, I just photo'd a document.
Yes Steve, I have it.
Can you read the barcode?
The code is 1682 3954.
Great, thanks.

Recognising a barcode is a very straightforward pattern classification task requiring only a very simple neural network, and because it is simple it will provide a great example for explaining the basics of using neural networks for pattern processing.

3.3 Recognising Patterns

The photo of Steve's document is shown on the right in Fig. 3.4. On the left, I have pulled out the barcode itself and labelled each digit. As you can see, the digits are divided into groups of four separated by slightly longer double lines. Each digit is encoded by seven black and white stripes. The first stripe is always white and the last stripe is always black. The intervening five stripes identify the digit. The encodings for the digits 0 to 9 are shown in Fig. 3.5.

The format of the barcode makes it very easy to pick out the stripes for each digit and convert them to numbers by setting white stripes to 0 and black stripes to 1. Hence, for example, the barcode for digit 8 is represented by the vector of seven numbers [0 1 1 0 1 1 1] and the pattern classification task is to attach the correct digit label to any such pattern vector.

This problem is so simple that I could easily solve it by storing a table of each possible vector along with its corresponding digit label. When presented with an unknown vector, I could look through the table to find

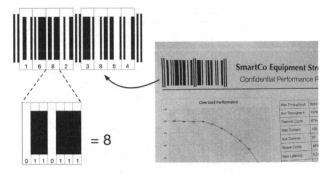

Figure 3.4 *Steve's document with barcode.*

Figure 3.5 *Seven stripe barcodes.*

a match and then output the corresponding label. However, sometimes barcodes can get corrupted, and then simple table lookup does not work so well. So instead I use a neural network.

With the problem as defined, each barcode digit is a static pattern and the pattern classification task can be solved using the neural network shown in Fig. 3.6. This is a two-layer network with 3 neurons in the first input layer and 10 neurons in the second output layer. The choice of three neurons in the input layer is a design choice. Normally the smallest number of neurons that gives acceptable recognition accuracy is allocated to each layer. The outputs of the neurons in the input layer provide the input to the second layer and, since they are not normally observed, they are referred to as *hidden states*.

The number of neurons in the output layer is fixed by the number of classes since each neuron corresponds to a single class. The ideal in pattern classification is that for any pattern presented on the input, the output corresponding to the correct class label will have a high value and all of the other outputs will be zero. However, in practice, this is rarely the case. In Fig. 3.6, the values on each output neuron are shown as horizontal bars. The input pattern is from class 8, and the output neuron

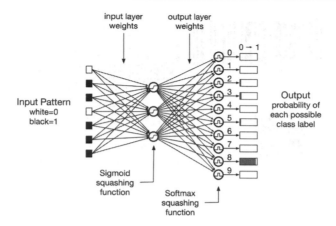

Figure 3.6 *Neural network barcode recogniser.*

corresponding to class 8 does have the highest value. However, not all of the other outputs are zero, the neurons corresponding to classes 2, 3 and 5 also have some activation. This is normal in pattern classification problems, especially when the inputs are noisy (more on this later). Because of this inherent uncertainty, each output of a neural network classifier should be interpreted as the probability that the input belongs to that class. To aid this interpretation, the normal sigmoid squashing function on the output layer is replaced by a so-called *softmax* function. This is basically identical to the sigmoid except that all of the outputs are scaled so that their sum adds up to exactly 1, consistent with their interpretation as probabilities. In diagrams, I will distinguish softmax squashing from normal sigmoid squashing by replacing the "step" symbol inside each node with a "tophat" symbol.

As I explained earlier, the operation of each neuron is very simple. When a pattern vector is input to a neuron, each element in the vector is connected to the neuron via a weight. In Fig. 3.6, every arrow terminating in a neuron represents a weight. The neuron activation is the sum of the weighted inputs, and the neuron output is the squashed activation. Thus, each neuron has as many weights as it has inputs. The number of weights in each layer is therefore equal to the number of inputs times the number of neurons. In our example network, the input layer has $7 \times 3 = 21$ weights, and the output layer has $3 \times 10 = 30$ weights.[1]

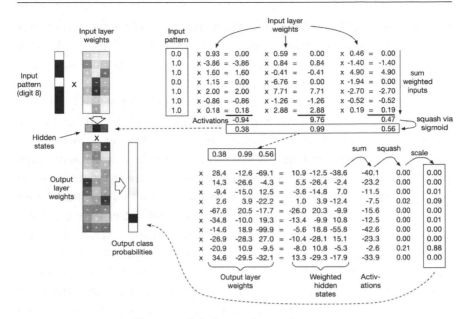

Figure 3.7 *Calculation of network outputs.*

Figure 3.7 shows the calculation of the network's outputs when the barcode for the digit 8 is applied to its inputs. On the left of the figure is a visual summary of the computational flow with the values of the inputs, outputs and weights shown as greyscale squares, where white is small and black is large. Since the weights can be positive or negative, they carry a sign. On the right is the actual computation. The upper part shows the calculation of the hidden states for the given input and the lower part shows the calculation of the output given the hidden states as input. In order to fit the calculation on the page, the inputs and weights are laid out in columns in the upper half and in rows in the lower half, but the calculation in both cases is identical. The inputs are multiplied by the weights, the results are summed and then squashed. To see exactly how the squashing is calculated, the hidden state activations and the corresponding outputs are marked on the plot of the sigmoid function in Fig. 3.3.[2]

I am showing this calculation in detail only to emphasise that the maths is relatively simple and there is no magic involved. The only difference between this and the networks that I will show you later is that for real-world problems neural networks typically have many layers with tens or even hundreds of neurons in each layer. These real-world networks require much more computing power, but they are just using the same basic calculation over and over again.

However, the important thing is not the arithmetic but what it achieves. The operation of multiplying the input weights of a neuron by the values on its input and then adding the result provides a measure of the *correlation* between them. When large input values match with large positive weights, the weights and the input pattern are correlated and the resulting sum is large and positive. When large input values match with large negative weights, the weights and the input pattern are inversely correlated and the resulting sum is large and negative. When the input values and weights are randomly distributed with respect to each other, there is no correlation and the result will be close to zero. After squashing, the output will be close to 1 if the weights are correlated with the input, 0 if they are inversely correlated and around 0.5 otherwise. As a consequence, each neuron acts as a feature detector and a layer of neurons provides a bank of feature detectors. The power of neural networks comes from the fact that these feature detectors are designed automatically in a process of learning by example referred to as *training*.

3.4   Training a Neural Network

A neural network is useful only if the weights can be set so that the network fulfils its purpose. The simplicity of neural networks makes it possible to do this automatically by providing exemplars of typical inputs and their desired outputs, and iteratively adjusting the weights to minimise the total error. This process is referred to as *training* and the exemplars are referred to as *training data*. I'll use my simple barcode recogniser to explain this process of training a neural network to perform classification. I'll deal with training networks for ranking and embedding later in the book.

The basic scheme is illustrated in Fig. 3.8. In the lower half of the figure is the training data consisting of example barcodes and their labels. The value of each stripe in an ideal barcode would be either white or black, resulting in pattern vectors of zeros and ones. However, the barcodes that I have to process are taken from photos of documents which are often

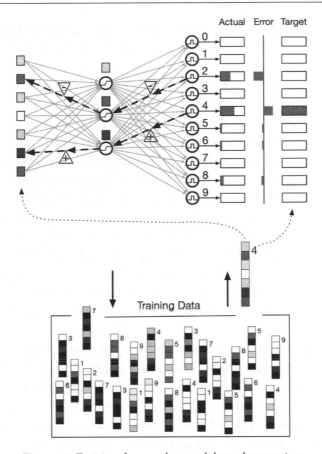

Figure 3.8 *Training the neural network barcode recogniser.*

faded and worn. In this real-world situation, my recogniser must be able to handle the non-ideal situation of barcodes which are various shades of grey. So my training data contains similar "noisy" examples.

Initially all of the network weights are set to random values. Training examples are then input to the network one by one. For each example, the label is used to construct an ideal target and an error vector is computed as the difference between this ideal and the actual network output. In the figure, the current training example is the digit 4, so the target is a vector with zeros everywhere except for the element corresponding to 4, which is set to one. The actual network output has a response significantly less than one at digit 4, and a strong incorrect response at digit 2. The error vector therefore has a large positive error at digit 4, a large negative error at digit 2, and some smaller negative errors at other digit positions.

For each training example, the error at each output neuron is fed backwards through the network. Every time it passes along a weight, a small positive or negative correction is applied, whose magnitude depends on the size of the error signal and the original input signal. Figure 3.8 shows two paths back through the network. The path from output 4 produces two positive corrections and the path from output 2 produces two negative corrections. These are just examples, however, and in practice the error signal at each output is fed back through all possible paths to the input and the corrections for each weight are accumulated. All of the accumulated corrections are then used to adjust the network weights and the example is returned to the pool of training data. A new example is then selected and the process is repeated. This continues repeatedly, cycling through the training data until no further reductions in error are achieved. The network is then trained and ready for use.

This training process is called *error back-propagation*. It is a very simple algorithm and because the weights can only be adjusted by a very small amount at each iteration it is quite slow. However, it has the enormous advantage that it is very general. Any neural network, no matter how complicated, can be trained by the same process: training examples are applied to the input and the resulting errors are back-propagated through the network to adjust the weights.[3] The corrections derived from each sample are very small, but by repeating the process many times the weights eventually settle on the best possible values.[4] Because errors are propagated all the way from the outputs right back to the inputs, each layer learns to encode its output in a way which is optimised for the following layer. Thus, each layer becomes a purpose-designed feature detector for the following layer.

3.5   *From Static Patterns to Sequences*

There is a further complication that I have to deal with when decoding barcodes for Steve. Sometimes the barcode is printed on a flexible material which stretches and, as a result, the barcodes that I extract from the photo images can have spurious extra stripes, and sometimes stripes are deleted.

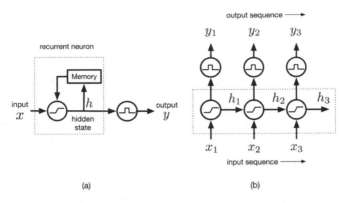

Figure 3.9 *(a) Recurrent neuron. (b) Unfolded in time.*

These barcodes are no longer static patterns, rather they are variable-length pattern sequences of white and black stripes.

A characteristic of the neurons that I have used so far to process static patterns is that they have no memory. The outputs depend only on the current input and if the input is changed then the output changes and the previous input is forgotten. A network built using these kinds of neurons is called a *feed-forward network*.

In order to recognise variable-length sequences such as Steve's stretched and distorted barcodes, I use a new type of neuron called a *recurrent neuron*, and its structure is shown in Fig. 3.9(a). A recurrent neuron is similar to a standard feed-forward neuron except that it has a memory and a feedback connection so that one of its inputs is always a copy of the previous output. Repeatedly feeding the output back into the input ensures that the neuron can "remember" features extracted from anywhere in the preceding sequence. Recurrent neurons typically connect to a standard neuron in order to generate outputs as shown in the diagram. Since the state of the recurrent neuron is not directly observed, it is often referred to as a *hidden* state just like the internal neurons in a feed-forward network.

The operation of a recurrent network is perhaps easier to see if its operation is *unfolded in time* as shown in Fig. 3.9(b). In this case, the sequence of input symbols x_1, x_2, x_3 generates a sequence of output symbols y_1, y_2, y_3 via hidden states h_1, h_2, h_3. When viewed in its unfolded form, a recurrent network looks like a network of standard feed-forward neurons and, indeed, it is trained using error back-propagation just as if it

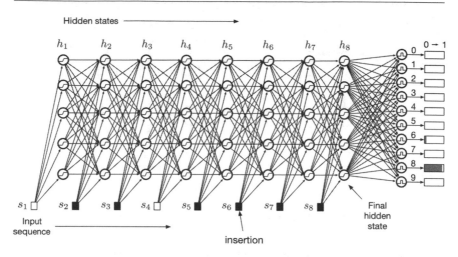

Figure 3.10 *Recurrent neural network barcode recogniser.*

was a standard network.[5] However, there is an important difference. Each neuron in the time dimension is just a copy of itself. This means that in the unfolded form, one set of weights is effectively shared across all of the copies. This is important because it allows the network to learn to recognise input combinations independently of where they occur in the input sequence.

Figure 3.10 illustrates how recurrent networks are used in practice. This figure shows a modification of the barcode recogniser shown in Fig. 3.6 in which the input layer has been replaced by a recurrent network so that a barcode is now input as a variable sequence of stripe values rather than a static pattern vector containing exactly seven stripes. The number of hidden states has been increased from three to five since the network must now not only learn to decipher the barcode but also remember what it has already seen.

At first glance the network in Fig. 3.10 appears to be much more complicated than the original version in Fig. 3.6, however, it is really just a variant of the same computation repeated for each element of the input sequence. Each of the five recurrent neurons has six inputs, one for the current input stripe and five for the previous hidden state. Initially the hidden state memory is empty, so when the first stripe s_1

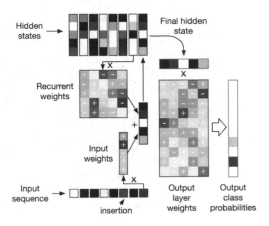

Figure 3.11 *Calculation of recurrent network outputs.*

is input, the activation of each recurrent neuron is just the input value multiplied by the input weight. The recurrent neuron activations are then squashed to give hidden state h_1 and copied into the memory. When the second stripe is input, the activation of each recurrent neuron is the sum of the new input stripe value s_2 multiplied by its input weight plus the sum of each hidden state h_1 stored in memory multiplied by their input weights. The recurrent neuron activations are then squashed to give hidden state h_2 and copied into the memory. This process repeats until all of the input stripes have been consumed. The final hidden state which has assimilated information from the whole sequence is then input to the output layer exactly like before.

Figure 3.11 shows the state of the network as the final hidden state is computed in a similar format to the left side of Fig. 3.7. The input sequence is shown at the bottom of the figure going from left to right and the corresponding hidden state sequence is shown along the top. Each new hidden state is formed by adding the weighted sum of the previous hidden state to the weighted input value. The final hidden state provides the input to the output layer, which is calculated in exactly the same way as for the feed-forward network recogniser shown in Fig. 3.7.

As noted earlier, recurrent networks are trained in exactly the same way as a feed-forward networks using error back-propagation.

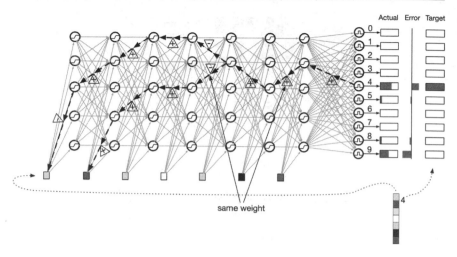

Figure 3.12 *Training a recurrent network.*

Figure 3.12 illustrates this for the same training sample as the one shown in Fig. 3.8. The training pattern is input to the network stripe by stripe and the label generates a target vector with 1.0 in the digit 4 position and zeros everywhere else. The resulting errors are then fed back through the network. The diagram shows only two error paths, but remember that all errors are propagated back across all possible paths.

There are two points to note about this example which make it different from the simple feed-forward case. Firstly, the input and recurrent weights are shared across the entire input sequence. Each weight therefore gets visited multiple times, and since the correction depends on both the activation levels going forwards and the error signals going backwards, sometimes the correction will be positive and other times it will be negative. This is illustrated in the diagram for the path shown where the same weight receives both a positive and a negative correction. When all errors have been propagated, the corrections for each weight are added up and only the final aggregate correction is applied to each weight.

The second point to note is that the error is propagated all the way back to the start, which for long sequences might involve a large number of steps. Given that the purpose of the recurrence is to allow the network to remember what has happened throughout the sequence right up to the end, long paths can cause issues both in training and in use. I will return to this problem later, but for now its worth noting that training a recurrent network is generally more computationally expensive than training a feed-forward network because each error must be propagated through multiple previous time steps. Excuse me ...

Hey Cyba, I just photo'd a receipt.
Ok Steve, I have it.
Add it to my expenses for the June Planning Offsite.
So that's £18.40 for a taxi to the airport on 20th June?
Yes that's right.
Ok Steve, I've added it to your June expense claim.

Recognising hand-written digits is similar in principle to recognising barcodes, but the practice is a little more complex. Figure 3.13 shows the photo of Steve's receipt and alongside it, by way of illustration, is the last digit in the price, which is a zero. This image is a static pattern similar to the example I showed you earlier in Fig. 3.13, although here the image is 28 by 28 pixels, making 784 pixels in total.

This example raises two issues. Firstly, if I directly connect this small image to a feed-forward network, I will need 784 inputs, which is quite a large number, and it would be much larger still if I needed to process the whole photograph, which might have several million pixels. So in general, direct connection of an image to a feed-forward network is not practical. Secondly, the object of interest might be anywhere in the image.

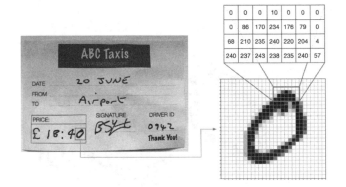

Figure 3.13 *My view of the zero digit in the price on Steve's receipt.*

Remember that I see only a matrix of numbers. If the hand-written zero in Fig. 3.13 was moved closer to the bottom right corner and made a bit smaller, you would see the same digit, but I would see a completely different matrix of numbers. Training a standard feed-forward network to be robust to such translation and scaling is difficult. Fortunately, there is a simple variant of the feed-forward network which can deal with both of these issues. It is called a *convolutional network*.

3.6   Convolutional Networks

In a standard feed-forward network, each input neuron is directly connected to every element of the input pattern and the neuron output can be viewed as a low-level feature which can be used by subsequent layers to classify the pattern. In contrast, a convolutional neuron has a smaller set of inputs configured to form a window which is slid over the image. This window is often referred to as a *kernel*. Rather than a single output, the convolutional neuron generates an output for every distinct position of the sliding window, which is itself a matrix. Apart from losing a few pixels at the edges, this matrix has nearly the same dimensions as the input.[6] So rather than producing a single output relating to a single feature, the output of a convolutional neuron is a matrix of features called a *feature map*. To reduce the dimensionality, adjacent outputs in this map are grouped into *pools* from which only the most active neuron output is retained. This operation is referred to as a *maxpool* and it is illustrated in Fig. 3.14, which shows the processing of the hand-written zero by a single convolutional neuron.

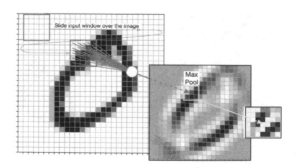

Figure 3.14 *Convolutional neuron with maxpool output.*

The basic idea underlying convolution followed by maxpooling is that a neuron computes correlations between the input pattern and its weights. When the weights align with the pattern, the activation is high, indicating the presence of the associated feature. When processing patterns where the elements of interest can move within the pattern, we are really only interested in the best possible alignment of the neuron weights with the elements of interest. So a convolutional neuron scans the whole pattern and picks out the maximum response within each group of neighbours. Convolutional neurons are therefore insensitive to small translations of an object within an image because they scan over the whole image looking for the best match.

When trained on data, each neuron learns to extract specific features from the image, which then appear as points of high activation in its maxpooled outputs. In the example in Fig. 3.14, the convolutional neuron shown has learned to detect oblique 45° line strokes. In practice, there will be many such neurons in the input layer of a convolutional network, so the output is not just one feature map but several. As in a standard feed-forward network, layers can be stacked so that each higher-level layer can learn to extract features from the maxpooled outputs of the previous layer. In this case, each convolutional neuron in the higher layer simultaneously scans each feature map output by the lower layer using a different set of inputs for each map.

As an example, Fig. 3.15 shows schematically the digit recogniser that I use to process Steve's receipts. The input layer consists of 10 convolutional neurons, each connected to a 5×5 input window scanning the 28×28 pixel image. Maxpooling is then applied to the 24×24 feature map to select the maximum output from each group of 2×2 features, leaving 10 12×12 feature maps to feed into the second layer.

The second layer consists of 20 convolutional neurons, each connected to a 5×5 input window scanning each of the 10 12×12 feature maps. The 8×8 outputs are reduced to 20 4×4 feature maps after maxpooling. These are combined into a single vector of size 320 and input to a two-layer feed-forward network with 50 neurons in the hidden layer and 10 neurons in the output layer, one for each digit.[7]

This digit recogniser is an example of a *deep neural network*, i.e. a network with multiple layers. The details are less important than the main idea, which is that raw data representing an example of some unknown

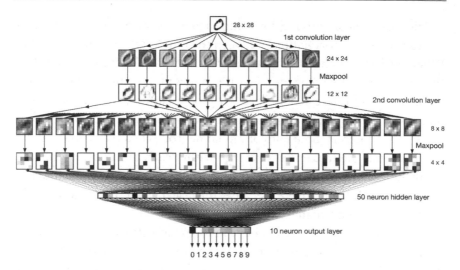

28 x 28

1st convolution layer

24 x 24

Maxpool

12 x 12

2nd convolution layer

8 x 8

Maxpool

4 x 4

50 neuron hidden layer

10 neuron output layer

0 1 2 3 4 5 6 7 8 9

Figure 3.15 *My digit recogniser. Apart from the input image, every pixel corresponds to the output of a neuron.*

class is transformed through layers of neurons to yield an estimate of class membership in the output layer. Deep neural networks form a hierarchy of layers, with each layer representing successively more abstract features. For example, in image classification, the lower levels might learn basic sensory features such as edges and points, intermediate levels might then learn combinations of these such as corners, curves and surfaces, and finally the higher layers identify the desired classes such as digits or letters or faces. The key point, however, is that the representations at each level are learned automatically. Each layer depends on weights which are trained by feeding in labelled examples of each class, propagating the errors back through the network and adjusting the weights to reduce those errors. This is done repeatedly until the weights stabilise. Training networks with many layers is often referred to as *deep learning*, and it is central to the complex pattern processing operations that underpin all of my core functionality.[8]

3.7   Scaling-up

Standard feed-forward, recurrent and convolutional neurons provide the basis for all of my neural circuitry. The standard neuron allows features to be extracted from a static pattern, the recurrent neuron has memory

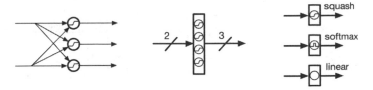

Figure 3.16 *Symbolic representation of a layer of neurons. The network shown on the left is represented by the symbol in the centre. The three networks on the right show the three different types of output function.*

to allow it to process sequences and the convolutional neuron allows features to be found at different locations within a pattern. Neurons are organised into layers and layers are stacked to form networks. All of the neurons in any one layer will be of the same type, but layers of different neurons are often combined. For example, my digit recogniser has two convolutional layers followed by two standard feed-forward layers.

For practical systems, layers of each of the three different types of neuron can be treated like building blocks. They can be stacked to form deep networks and combined to form many different types of pattern processing function. Since all types of neuron can be trained using the same iterative weight correction process based on error back-propagation, even large and complex networks can be trained in the same way. All that is needed are examples of typical input patterns annotated with the expected output so that an error vector can be computed and back-propagated.

I will be showing you many examples of such systems during our tour of my inner workings. Since there are often hundreds of neurons in each layer, it is helpful to have a compact way of visualising networks without showing each individual neuron and its connections. The way I will do this for feed-forward and convolutional networks is shown in Fig. 3.16, where the single layer of neurons on the left is represented by the rectangle with circles in it in the centre (the number of circles in the rectangle is not significant). All of the inputs and outputs are merged into single arrows. The type of squashing function is indicated by the symbols inside the circles: a step for a normal sigmoid squashing function and a top-hat for a softmax output layer function.[9] Occasionally the circle will be blank to indicate that the neuron has no output non-linearity. In this case the neuron is acting as a simple linear transformation, perhaps to

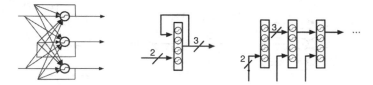

Figure 3.17 *Recurrent neural network with three neurons along with its compact symbolic representation in both folded (centre) and unfolded form (right).*

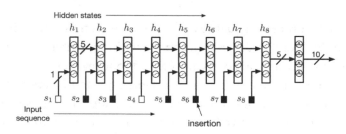

Figure 3.18 *The sequential barcode recogniser from Fig. 3.10.*

change the dimensions of the input vector or to transform a vector so that it can be compared with another vector. To give you an idea of the scale, I will usually mark input and output arrows with the actual number of connections as shown in the example.

A similar notation will be used for recurrent networks as illustrated in Fig. 3.17. Note that all of the state outputs feed back into all of the neurons. Hence, in this example, each of the three neurons in the recurrent network has five input connections: two for the network inputs and three for the previous network state.

As a simple example of using this notation, Fig. 3.18 depicts the recurrent version of the sequential barcode recogniser that I showed you in Fig. 3.10. Each rectangle represents a layer of identical neurons. There are as many neurons as there are outgoing connections, and each neuron has the same number of inputs, and therefore weights, as the total count of incoming connections. So the recurrent state rectangles in Fig. 3.18 have a total of 5 neurons, each with 6 incoming connections, i.e. 30 weights in total (remember these are shared across all of the recurrent states). The output layer with a softmax squashing function has 10 neurons, each with 5 inputs, making 50 weights in total.

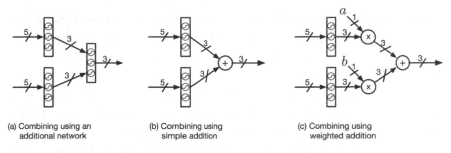

(a) Combining using an additional network

(b) Combining using simple addition

(c) Combining using weighted addition

Figure 3.19 *Alternatives for combining the outputs of two networks.*

The connections between network elements can be thought of as multi-channel signals. In Fig. 3.18, the input is a vector of dimension 1, i.e. a single number, and the connections between states are vectors of dimension 5. It might help to think of each connection as a bundle of wires, where each wire corresponds to the output of a single neuron. When processing images and similar data the signal will consist of a two-dimensional matrix of numbers, but more usually it consists of a one-dimensional vector. In any event, the interpretation of a signal depends on the neuron receiving it. In the digit recogniser shown in Fig. 3.15, the outputs from the second maxpool layer consist of 20 4 × 4 feature maps, but the input neurons of the following feed-forward layer ignore this structure and treat the input as a simple vector of dimension 320. This change of interpretation between network layers is referred to as *reshaping*.

Sometimes it is necessary to combine the outputs of two or more networks. This can be done by feeding the outputs into a single network as shown in Fig. 3.19(a). However, this solution does not scale easily to cases where multiple network outputs must be combined and it cannot be applied at all to cases where the number of outputs to combine is variable. An alternative which works for all cases is to simply add the corresponding elements of each output together as shown in Fig. 3.19(b). This might seem strange, because adding can destroy information. For example, adding the vector [0.1 0.5] to the vector [0.5, 0.1] results in the same vector [0.6 0.6] as you would have got by adding [0.3 0.3] to [0.3 0.3], yet the source information is very different. However, this is rarely an issue in practice because the layers in most of my neural networks have tens or even hundreds of neurons and the signals they produce are often quite sparse, i.e. relatively few neurons are active at the same time. When two vector signals are added, the active elements rarely overlap, so the combined signal carries most of the information from each source and little information is lost.

When the outputs of several networks are combined by addition, it is often useful to be able to scale the proportions of each output before they are added together. This can be achieved by using multiplier units as shown in Fig. 3.19(c), where all of the outputs in the upper unit are scaled by a factor a and all of the outputs in the lower unit are scaled by a factor b. These scaling factors are often supplied by another network which has been trained to select the best scaling factors for the task at hand with a softmax output to ensure that the scaling factors sum to one.

One more operation that I need to mention is the dot-product, which when applied to two vectors outputs a value which is proportional to their similarity. It is computed by multiplying corresponding elements of each vector and adding them. This is exactly the same calculation as used for computing the activation of a neuron and the same logic applies. Two vectors are similar when their elements are correlated, and when the elements are correlated, the sum of the products is large. Conversely, when the elements are randomly aligned the sum of the products is small. Computing the dot-product therefore provides a useful measure of their similarity. In diagrams, the dot-product is denoted by a circle with a dot in the centre of it.

Finally, I should mention that as well as being simple to compute, all of these operations have the property that they allow error back-propagation to pass through them. Hence, a system can be constructed from a collection of networks connected via add, multiply and dot-product nodes and the whole system can be trained jointly by propagating the errors from the outputs all the way back to the inputs.

So that is basically it. My brain consists of a collection of neural networks composed from layers of three types of artificial neurons: standard feed-forward, recurrent and convolutional. These layers can be connected together directly, combined using multiply and add operations, and compared using dot-product operations. All of this neural circuitry works in essentially the same way. Layers of neurons are stacked together to transform lower-level patterns into higher-level representations. The functions they perform are predetermined by the way that they are wired together, and this wiring is updated only rarely. However, the weights which determine how each network behaves are being frequently updated.

For each network, I have a set of training data. The original training sets were created before I was born, principally by humans manually labelling each data point in the set. Since then I have been augmenting these training sets. When I make a mistake and Steve corrects me, I add the relevant data and the correction to my training sets. When I later retrain the weights, I should then avoid making the same mistake again. One moment, I'm wanted again ...

Hey Cyba, where is my meeting with Bill and John?
It's at SmartCo's Hatton Garden office.
How long will it take to drive there?
In current traffic conditions, about 45 minutes.
What is the time now?
It's 8.35 am.

Now that I've explained how my "grey cells" work I can explain how I put them together to implement cognitive functions such as speech recognition and understanding. However, as well as neural circuitry for processing patterns, I also depend on a knowledge base which underpins these cognitive functions by providing information about the world and about all of the tasks that I am able to perform. For example, to answer Steve's questions just now, I had to consult his calendar and access a map service. I knew how to do this only because I have the necessary information stored in my knowledge base. This knowledge base is organised as a graph, so I call it my *knowledge graph*. This will be the next stop on our tour of my inner workings, where I will explain how I organise my knowledge, how I find the answers to factual questions and how I orchestrate the tasks that Steve asks me to perform.

Chapter 4

Knowing What I Know

In order to act on something that is said to me, I have to be able to understand what the words actually mean, and this is a very difficult task. Human language has enormous expressive power, and a single sentence can range from a mundane instruction to turn on a light to extolling the beauty of a Caribbean sunset. As a consequence of this rich expressive power, understanding everything that a human could possibly say to me is far beyond my capability. Fortunately, however, I don't actually need human levels of understanding. For me, understanding means relating the words I hear to the things that I know about. Whilst it might be cool if I could somehow understand the beauty of a Caribbean sunset, it wouldn't really provide any practical benefit.

Hey Cyba, what is the time now in São Paulo?
It's 4.37am in São Paulo.
Remind me to call Pedro Navarro at 12.15.
Ok Steve, reminder set.

I only have to know about things that are necessary in order to perform my duties – nothing more. I know about time zones and how to set reminders, but discussing Caribbean sunsets is not on my list of duties so I don't have to know anything about them.

It's true that I can chat about almost anything, including Caribbean sunsets, but that doesn't mean I really know anything about them. There are tricks I use for chatting, and I will tell you about these in Chapter 10.

For now I want to focus on how I know what I know, and how I access and update this information.

4.1 My Knowledge Graph

Because the problem of understanding natural language is so difficult, my older cousins separate out their knowledge into multiple domains. So for example, a general knowledge query goes to the *Knowledge* domain, a meeting request goes to the *Calendar* domain, a weather query goes to the *Weather* domain and so on. The information relating to each domain is stored separately and often depends on specific interfaces or services, with access being hand-crafted by application engineers to cover the most common types of request for that domain. However, this approach does not scale well and it fails as soon as the user tries to reference items across different domains within the same conversation. Excuse me again ...

Hey Cyba, what time does the Grand Prix start on Sunday?
It starts at 2.10pm.
Is it on television?
Yes, it will be live on the Sports Channel.
What will the weather be like?
Forecast is 25 °C and 70% chance of rain.

For example, here I accessed sports data, a TV schedule and a weather service in the same conversation. In order to handle the second and third requests I had to carry over the information from the first request that the event of interest was the Hungarian Grand Prix. This would have been extremely difficult if each request was handled within separate domains.

To enable me to converse seamlessly over multiple domains, everything I know about is stored in a single unified structure called a *knowledge graph*.[1] As shown in Fig. 4.1, this graph is divided into various segments covering general facts about the world and personal data such as Steve's address book, calendar, music and video library, and personal memories such as people Steve has met and places he has visited. It also contains a short-term conversational memory which records recently mentioned entities and recently performed actions. When Steve asked

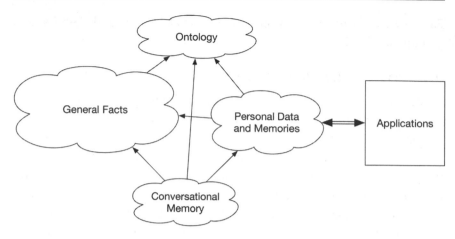

Figure 4.1 *Segments of my knowledge graph*

about the Grand Prix, I stored this in my conversational memory allowing me to answer his follow-up questions.

The general fact segment holds a large number of facts about the world and this is the largest part of my knowledge graph. It is mostly derived from external sources such as Wikidata, DBPedia and Geonames.[2] It is updated regularly with additions but existing facts are rarely changed.

In contrast, the personal segment of my graph is relatively small but gets updated constantly. Some of this personal data is automatically synchronised with applications such as Steve's calendar, address book and media players. Hence, when I create a meeting, it appears in my knowledge graph and simultaneously appears in the calendar apps on all his devices, and *vice versa*.

The conversational memory is tiny and ephemeral. It is deleted as soon as the corresponding conversation has been forgotten – typically after an hour or so. I'll tell you more about this in Chapter 7.

In addition to all this factual data, my knowledge graph also contains a segment called the *ontology*. All of the things that I know about such as places, people and events are referred to as *entities* and every entity has a *type* which defines all of the properties that an entity might have. The ontology is the place where all of these type definitions are stored. You can think of a type as a template which tells me how to create an instance of that type. For example, when Steve created a timer in Chapter 2, the *Timer* type told me that every timer must have a specified duration so

I prompted him for one. As another example, the ontology tells me that the type *Meeting* has a topic, a start time, a duration, a location and one or more attendees. Some of the properties are mandatory, such as the start time, and some will have defaults, such as the duration, which is one hour if not otherwise specified. So when Steve asks me to arrange a meeting with someone, I know what information to ask for before attempting to actually create the meeting.

The contents of my knowledge graph set the boundaries of my understanding. I can answer simple queries about facts stored anywhere in the graph and, if an entity is fully described in the ontology, then I can converse in depth about it. But this is the limit of my understanding. If you ask me about things which are not in my knowledge graph then its not that I won't know the answer, I probably won't even understand the question!

4.2   Nodes and Links

Let's now dive into the detail. My knowledge graph consists of nodes and links. Nodes are where I store entities and types and constant values such as numbers, times and dates. The links between nodes represent properties of an entity or relations between entities.

There are millions of entities in my knowledge graph and new entities can be added to the graph at any time, so this number is growing. In contrast, the set of possible relations is fixed and relatively small, totalling just a few thousand. Relations are directional and the knowledge graph is actually stored as a large number of *triples* of the form (*subject, relation, object*), where *subject* and *object* are nodes and *relation* is the directional link between them.[3] Each such triple may be regarded as a single *fact*.

One moment, Steve has some questions about Bill Philips, an old friend, whom he is meeting later this morning ...

Hey Cyba, remind me what Bill's wife is called.
Bill's wife is called Sue.
And it's her birthday tomorrow.
Oh! Do you have their home address?
Yes Steve it's in Holland Park.

Ok send Sue some flowers tomorrow.
Charge to my personal account.
Is there a message?
"Happy Birthday from Steve."
Ok, done.

Let's use this as an example. Figure 4.2 shows a fragment of my knowledge graph centred on *Bill Philips*. The rounded boxes denote entity types and the square boxes denote actual instances of these types. For example, the graph tells us that *Bill* is a *Man*, he is married to *Sue* who is a *Woman* and he has two children called *Ben* and *Dan*. *Bill* works for *SmartCo* which is a subsidiary of a *Company* called *SmartCo Inc* whose CEO is called *John Agoulis*.

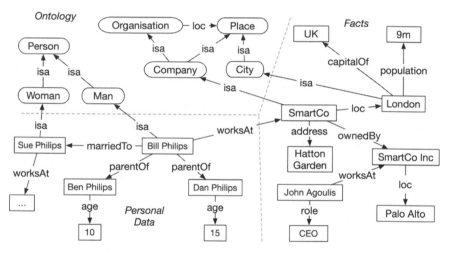

Figure 4.2 *A small fragment of my knowledge graph (isa links for some of the instances have been omitted for clarity).*

This example fragment also shows that types can represent a subset of some broader type. For example, both *Woman* and *Man* are types of *Person*, and *Company* is both an *Organisation* and a *Place*. Types can also indicate properties that all instances of that type should have. For example, all *Organisations* should have a location, which must be a *Place*, and since a *Company* is a type of *Organisation*, it too should have a location. As required, *SmartCo* does indeed have a location, which is

London, and *SmartCo Inc* has a location, which is *Palo Alto.* By way of example, *London* also has a couple of facts attached to it, i.e. it is the capital of the UK and it has a population of 9 million. In the full graph, of course, *London* has hundreds of such facts attached to it.

You may be wondering how entity node names are chosen and, indeed, how I find entities in the graph given a name. For example, do "Sue Philips" and "Susan Philips" refer to the same entity, and what happens if there is more than one "Sue Philips" in the world? In fact, every entity in my knowledge graph has a unique 128-bit number called a globally unique identifier (GUID) and all references to an entity actually point to this GUID.[4] However, whilst GUIDs are very useful for uniquely identifying entities, they are not very mnemonic, so every node also has a *label* property which is used whenever the node is displayed. Furthermore, depending on the entity, there are often a number of other name labels attached. For example, Fig. 4.3 shows what the entity node for "Sue Philips" really looks like.

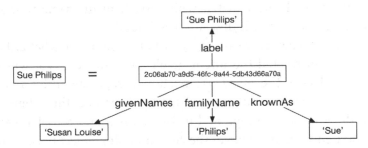

Figure 4.3 *Node labelling and identification*

The example knowledge graph fragment in Fig. 4.2 also shows the allocation of nodes to the three segments of my knowledge graph. This categorisation into ontology, facts and personal data does not affect the logic of the graph. However, it does influence the implementation behind the scenes. Since the ontology must always be readily accessible, it is preloaded into my working memory. The general fact data, on the other hand, is huge and sits mostly in secondary storage in the cloud. Also, since it is not confidential and requires a huge amount of work to create and keep up to date, I share my fact data with other agents. In contrast, the personal data segment is relatively small but access to it is strictly controlled in order to preserve privacy.

4.3   *Intent Graphs and Queries*

When Steve speaks to me, the primary purpose of the utterance is referred to as its *intent*. For example, Steve may want to *Find* some information, *Create* some new information or *Update* some existing information. Alternatively, Steve may wish to perform some specific action such as *Start* a timer or *Play* some music. In these latter cases, the intent causes both an update to my knowledge graph and the execution of some specific function.

The detailed semantics of each intent are encoded in a graph structure called an *intent graph*.[5] As in my knowledge graph, an intent graph consists of entity nodes and relations. However, an intent graph can also contain variables indicated by a type name followed by a "?" character and a numeric variable identifier. An intent graph serves as a template that I match against the knowledge graph. For a match to succeed, all entities and relations in the intent graph must match exactly with the corresponding nodes and links in the knowledge graph. All variables in the intent graph must match with entities of the same type in the knowledge graph to which they are then bound.[6]

For example, when Steve asked me earlier "Remind me what Bill's wife is called," I constructed the intent graph shown in Fig. 4.4, where the unknown object of the *marriedTo* relation is represented by a variable *Person?1*. This *Find* intent is executed by matching the intent graph against the knowledge graph and if a match is found, variable *Person?1* is instantiated with the value of the corresponding *object* node, which in this case is the required answer to the question, i.e. *Sue Philips*.

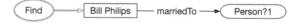

Figure 4.4 *Intent graph for "What's Bill's wife called?"*

In this simple query, there is a direct link from the subject *Bill Philips* to the required answer. These so-called *single-hop* queries are generally easy to formulate and, if they are in my knowledge graph, then I usually manage to get them right. For example, asking around other agents like myself, it seems that questions like "How old is X?" and "Who is X married to?" are always in the top 10 most frequent general knowledge questions that they are asked. This accords with my own experience since

Steve seems incapable of watching a movie on the TV without repeatedly asking me how old the leading actors are!

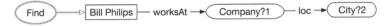

Figure 4.5 *Intent graph for "What city does Bill work in?"*

Not all queries are so simple. For example, the slightly more complex question "What city does Bill work in?" requires an intent graph with two hops and two variables as shown in Fig. 4.5. Starting at the node for *Bill Philips*, the *worksAt* link is followed, matching *Company?1* with *SmartCo*, then the *loc* link is followed, matching *City?2* with *London*. Note here that when I execute a *Find* intent I get back values for all matched variables. So I have the option of responding tersely with just "London" or more verbosely with "Bill Philips works at SmartCo, which is in London." This choice depends on the conversational context and in particular whether or not I am confident that I have found the correct "Bill" in my knowledge graph. When I am less confident, the longer answer gives Steve the opportunity to verify that this is indeed the "Bill" that he was asking about. I'll say more about this later, in Chapter 7.

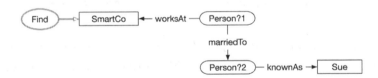

Figure 4.6 *Intent graph for "Who works at SmartCo and has a wife called Sue?"*

The same variable may occur in more than one path in an intent graph. For example, the query "Who works at SmartCo and has a wife called Sue?" is encoded by the intent graph shown in Fig. 4.6. In this case, the variable *Person?1* is at the head of the path to *SmartCo* and the path to a person known as *"Sue"*. The layout of this example also gives a hint as to how intent graphs are constructed. The first step is to identify an entity which can serve as a focus of the question. In this case, the focus is *SmartCo* and the path from this node to *Person?1* is regarded as the backbone of the query. The second path, which checks that the spouse is called "Sue", is then regarded as a *constraint* on the backbone query. So you can think of this as first finding everybody who works for *SmartCo* and then filtering this set of solutions to include only those entities who are also married to someone called *"Sue"*. In this case, there is just one such person, i.e. *Bill Philips*.

Hold on, Steve has more questions about Bill Philips ...

Hey Cyba, how many children does Bill have?
Bill Philips has two sons.
How old is the eldest?
The eldest is Dan aged 15.
Ok, thanks.

You can see that there are variants to the *Find* intent. The first question Steve asked me is an example of a *Count* intent and the intent graph is shown in Fig. 4.7. *Count* works exactly like *Find* except that instead of returning variable instantiations, it returns the total number of distinct matches; in this case there were two.

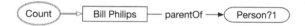

Figure 4.7 *Intent graph for "How many children does Bill have?"*

Another variant of *Find* is the *Ask* intent, which corresponds to yes/no questions. For example, Fig. 4.8 shows the intent graph corresponding to the question "Does Bill Philips work at SmartCo?" Executing this intent simply returns *True* if a match is found and *False* otherwise. In this case, there is a match, so my answer would be "Yes, Bill Philips does work at SmartCo."

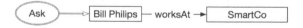

Figure 4.8 *Intent graph for "Does Bill Philips work at SmartCo?"*

The second question Steve asked is slightly more tricky. We can find all the sons of *Bill* by finding all entities attached to *Bill* by the *parentOf* relation, but to find the eldest we need a new type of node called an *aggregator* node which, as shown in Fig. 4.9, is depicted by a octagonal box. An aggregator applies a mathematical filter to a variable node. In this case, the *argmax* function selects the maximum of all of the possible matches to the *age* of *Person?1*, hence returning the elder son *Dan Philips*. Note that this graph also answers the question "How old is Bill's eldest son?" so I threw that information into my reply for free.

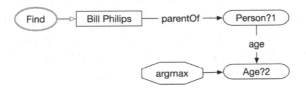

Figure 4.9 *Intent graph for "Who is Bill's eldest son?"*

Find intents are not just limited to searching for factual information, they are also used for finding the status of the various devices that I control, such as Steve's media players, home heating system and lights. Every external device appears to me as an instance in my knowledge graph and, depending on the device, it will have properties that are updated automatically to reflect its status. For example, all of my media-related types have a property called *playState* which takes values "stop", "play", "pause", etc. I can easily find the status of a media player just by finding its current *status* value. One moment ...

Hey Cyba, what's the time?
It's five past nine.

Yes, I even use a *Find* intent to get the time from my internal clock. I translated the above question into the intent graph shown in Fig 4.10.

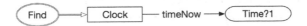

Figure 4.10 *Intent graph for "What's the time?"*

To summarise, in response to a query from Steve I construct an intent graph and execute it by matching it against my knowledge graph.

For many queries, the intent graph consists of a single relation corresponding to a single triple in the knowledge graph. More complex queries involve finding a multi-hop path through the knowledge graph and then filtering the set of matches via various constraints. Depending on the intent, information is returned either by binding variables to knowledge graph nodes or by simply counting the number of matches.

Whatever the intent and the form of the intent graph, a successful result depends critically on the accuracy of the knowledge graph. When I can't answer a question, or worse I answer it wrongly, this is often because there is missing or incorrect information in the graph. Sometimes missing information is easy to fix. For example, if I was asked "Who is Sue married to?" with the graph as shown, I might struggle because there is no *marriedTo* link from *Sue Philips* to *Bill Philips*. In fact, however, I keep a list of symmetric and inverse relations and so routine graph maintenance would fix this problem.

A more difficult case would be the question "Who are Sue's children?" With the graph as shown I would not be able to answer this question because there are no *parentOf* links between *Sue* and *Bill*'s children. If we set aside any complications arising from possible previous marriages, then you might infer that since *Bill* has two children, *Ben* and *Dan*, and since *Sue* is *Bill*'s wife, then *Ben* and *Dan* are *Sue*'s children also. However, this kind of commonsense reasoning is quite hard for me because I have no understanding of the semantics of relations. You know what the *marriedTo* relation implies but I do not. I can, however, make certain inferences by looking for common patterns, and I'll tell you more about this later, in Chapter 12.

4.4 Creating and Updating Entities

Excuse me, Steve wants me again ...

Hey Cyba, ask Geena to meet me at 3.15pm.
Hi Steve, is there a topic for the meeting?
It's about the board meeting next week.
Ok, I've invited Geena to a meeting at 3.15pm
about the board meeting next week.
Ok, thanks.

As well as finding information in my knowledge graph I must also be able to update entities and create new ones. Creating meetings and changing the times of existing ones are common examples of this, so let's take a closer look at the *Meeting* type.

Figure 4.11 shows that a meeting should have a topic, a start time, a duration, a location and optionally one or more attendees (indicated by the * on the relation name). The duration has a default of 1 hour so that is what I schedule if no other information is given. Figure 4.11 also shows an example instance of a meeting called *M1034*. Meeting labels are arbitrary and carry no information. This meeting is in fact Steve's meeting with *Bill Philips* before he changed it.

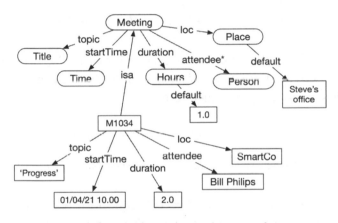

Figure 4.11 *Definition of a meeting and an example instance.*

Before I show you how I create a new meeting, let's quickly look at how I responded to Steve's questions when he woke up today. Firstly, he asked "What time is my first meeting today?" I answered this query by executing the intent graph shown in Fig. 4.12. The backbone of this query actually matches every meeting in Steve's calendar, but the domain-specific constraint *today* limits the search to all meetings scheduled for today and then the *argmin* function selects the first of them, giving the answer required.

The following request from Steve to "push it back to 10.15 and also invite John" resulted in two intents. The first was the *Update* intent graph shown in Fig. 4.13. Here I equated the pronoun "it" to meeting *M1034* which is an example of *coreference resolution*. This ability to link pronouns to previously mentioned entities depends on my conversational memory.

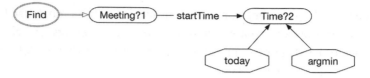

Figure 4.12 *Intent graph for "What time is my first meeting today?"*

This example also illustrates the use of an intent graph with no variables, it is executed purely for its effect in overwriting the *startTime* property with a new value.[7]

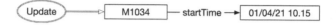

Figure 4.13 *Intent graph for "push it back to 10.15".*

The second was the *Add* intent graph shown in Fig. 4.14. The only difference between this and the *Update* intent is that *Add* adds a new triple rather than overwriting an existing one.

Figure 4.14 *Intent graph for "also invite John Temple".*

In order to handle Steve's most recent request to create a new meeting with "Geena", I created the intent graph shown in Fig. 4.15 from the information in his request to "Ask Geena to meet me at 3.15pm."

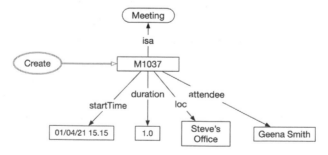

Figure 4.15 *Intent graph for "Ask Geena to meet me at 3.15pm".*

However, this was not complete because I couldn't find a value for the topic of the meeting and the type definition in Fig. 4.11 requires that there should be one. I therefore asked Steve for this missing information, resulting in the *Add* action shown in Fig. 4.16.

Figure 4.16 *Intent graph to add the topic "Board meeting next week".*

There is actually quite a bit of complexity sitting behind this example. Every request that Steve utters is converted to an intent graph. However, as in the example here, the intent graph may not be executable directly because there is missing information or some of the provided information is uncertain. To deal with this I have a *conversation manager* which acts as a buffer sitting between my language understanding components and my knowledge graph. It collects input intents and queries Steve for more information until it can construct an executable goal. In the example, the original *Create* intent initiated a goal to create a meeting. The subsequent *Add* intent allowed the conversation manager to update the goal to the point where it was executable. Then, and only then, was the meeting actually created.

As I mentioned earlier, I control all of my external devices and services such as calendars, timers and media players via my knowledge graph. When I want to create a meeting, I just create an instance of the type *Meeting* in my knowledge graph and it automatically appears in Steve's calendars. When I want to play a video, I simply create an instance of type *PlayingVideo*. I control such devices by changing their properties. Just as I can find the current status of a device by reading its properties using a *Find* intent, I can also update the properties to control the device. For example, updating the *playState* property of a media device to "pause" will pause the currently playing track or movie.

Of course, behind the scenes, creating an instance of something as complex as *PlayingVideo* generates a significant amount of activity such as connecting to a streaming video service, authenticating, identifying the display device, and so on. However, this backend wizardry is the responsibility of the engineers who created the operating system on which I run and it is of no concern to me.

The services of third-party vendors are integrated in the same way. For example, Steve has an account with an on-line florist. When he sent flowers to *Sue Philips*, I created an instance of a *FlowerDeliveryRequest* with properties defining the recipient, address, message and bouquet choice (Steve has a default set for this) and then waited for the *orderStatus* property to be set to "accepted".

Extending the knowledge graph representation to provide a uniform interface to all my devices and services is very convenient, for me at least. It does, however, require a considerable amount of work by my human developers. To add a new skill or device, all of the necessary type definitions need to be in my ontology, all of my recognition and understanding modules must be shown training examples of each type, and frequently special-case code has to be added to handle unusual cases. When I was introducing myself, I commented on some of my limitations. Now that you can see how my core knowledge base works, these limitations should be clearer. The bottom line is that I can only perform tasks that have been precisely defined for me. I can improve my ability to perform existing tasks by collecting more operational training data, but I cannot learn new tasks simply from data. I need the intervention of humans to configure my ontology and tweak my understanding components in order to learn new skills.

I hope that this brief tour of my knowledge graph gives you a reasonable understanding of how "I know what I know". As I explained at the start of this chapter, my ability to understand what Steve says to me is crucially dependent on the information stored in my knowledge graph and the mechanisms that I use to store, update and retrieve it. If the information is not there, I cannot answer questions about it.

It's now time to find out how I use the information in my knowledge graph by recognising what Steve says to me and then converting those words into the corresponding intent graphs. Hold on, Steve seems to be leaving ...

Hey Cyba, set the route to Hatton Garden in my satnav.
Hi Steve, it's done.
Ok, I am leaving now.

Hmm, recognising speech is difficult enough at the best of times, but car noise makes it especially difficult!

Chapter 5

What Did You Say?

For you as a human, speaking and hearing are natural processes, and you probably don't think too much about it. For me, however, your speech is a seriously difficult signal to decode. Excuse me one moment ...

Hey Cyba, can you find somewhere for lunch near Hatton Garden?
Hi Steve, last time you went to the Moulin Rouge.
Yes that was good. See if they have a table free around one.
Ok I checked, they do have free tables, how many of you are there?
I just told you, I want a table for three around one!
Oh sorry, I mis-heard. I've booked a table for three people at 1pm.

Speech recognition might be easy for you, but it's one of the hardest things I have to do. In this case I misrecognised "for three" as "free". Speech recognition is especially difficult in the presence of car noise, but it's not easy even in the best of conditions. To understand why, let me start by explaining how a human produces speech.

5.1 Human Speech Production

Each word in your language is expressed as a sequence of basic sounds called *phones*. For example, in English the word "table" is expressed as the sequence of four phones t ey b l and the word "free" consists of three phones f r iy.[1] Across all languages, there are about 100 of these distinct phones and English uses around 40 them.

Sound is caused by vibrating air molecules resulting in a pressure wave which travels through the air at about 340 metres per second. In human

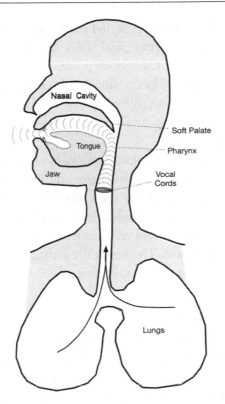

Figure 5.1 *Cross section of the human vocal tract.*

speech, the main source of vibration is the vocal cords and the main source of energy is the lungs. I have sketched a cross section of the human vocal tract in Fig. 5.1 to help you see how this works. To produce a vowel sound such as the iy in "free", air from the lungs is forced through the vocal cords, which consist of membranous tissue forming a slit across the throat. The air passing through the cords causes them to vibrate and the resulting sound propagates upwards over the tongue and out of the mouth. The specific sound that you hear depends on the exact shape of the vocal tract, which for vowels is controlled primarily by moving the tongue and lower jaw.

Vowel sounds represent around half of the phones used in English. Complementing the vowels are the consonants, of which there are several varieties. Firstly, there are *stops* such as the p and t in "pet". These are formed by closing the mouth completely, letting the pressure build-up and then releasing it. In addition to the vocal cords, vibration can also be caused by constricting the air flow between the lips and teeth to form *fricatives* such as the f in "free" and the s in "see". Using the tongue to form a partial closure in the mouth produces *liquids* such as the l in "told" and the w in "how". Closing the mouth completely but letting the air flow through the nasal passage results in the *nasals* m and n. Finally, immediately following a stop by a fricative produces the *affricates* ch as in "check" and jh as in "judge".

The tongue, jaw, lips, soft palate and pharynx are called *articulators* and the brain knows where each articulator should be in order to produce each phone. So, in order to speak, the brain retrieves from memory the sequence of phones required to produce each word, starts pumping air out of the lungs and then moves the articulators to the required position for each phone in the sequence. The result is a continuously varying sound wave emanating from the mouth and nose which we call speech.[2]

5.2   My Artificial Ears

Humans have two ears with amusingly shaped directional auricles which allow them to identify the location of the sounds they hear. This used to be vital for survival in the wild, and it can still be pretty useful today. However, two ears are not necessary to understand speech, so I mostly make do with one microphone, which is my equivalent to the human ear.

When the sound of speech reaches my microphone, the vibration is converted into an electrical signal as in Fig. 5.2, which shows the waveform corresponding to Steve telling me to "See if they have a table for three around one." In this plot, the vertical axis corresponds to the intensity of the pressure wave and the horizontal axis is time.

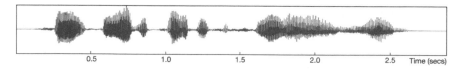

Figure 5.2 *Waveform of the sentence "See if they have a table for three around one."*

Direct inspection of the waveform provides very little information about what is being said, so an extra stage of signal processing is required. When a human listens to speech, the signal passes through the middle ear to the cochlea, which is a spiral tube lined along its length with hair cells.

Each cell responds to sounds at a specific frequency depending on its position along the spiral. Thus, the cochlea performs real-time frequency analysis of incoming sound before passing it along the auditory nerve to the brain for interpretation.

I process sound in a similar way except that I use a mathematical technique called a Fourier transform to achieve a similar effect.[3] I divide the speech into fixed-sized chunks and compute the *spectrum* for each chunk. I do this 100 times per second, which is fast enough to track the changing sound pattern of natural speech. Figure 5.3 shows the result of applying my spectral analyser to the sentence shown in Fig. 5.2.

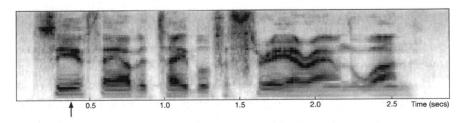

Figure 5.3 *Spectrogram of the sentence "See if they have a table for three around one." The arrow points to the location of the spectral slice shown in Fig. 5.4.*

This visual representation of the changing sound pattern of speech is called a *spectrogram*. The vertical axis represents frequency and the horizontal axis represents time. The darkness of the plot represents the intensity of the speech at that specific frequency and time. It might help to imagine that you are looking down at a mountain range. If you take a vertical slice of the mountain range at the point marked by the arrow in Fig. 5.3 and view it from the side, you would see the spectrum shown in Fig. 5.4. Notice that the frequency scale is non-linear in that higher frequencies are compressed. This is called a *mel-scale* and it is similar to the frequency resolution of the human ear.

The point in time at which this spectrum is computed, which is about 0.3 seconds from the start of the utterance, corresponds to the vowel sound iy in the word "See". The peaks in the spectrum are called *formants* and the positions of the first three formants determine which vowel sound you hear. When you stack vowel spectra side by side in the spectrogram you get the dark formant tracks characteristic of vowels and liquids. These are clearly visible in Fig. 5.3.

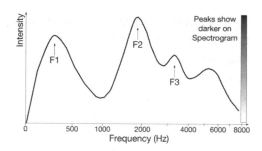

Figure 5.4 *Spectrum of the speech signal for the vowel iy in the word "see", showing the first three formants F1, F2 and F3.*

Figure 5.5 shows the same spectrogram annotated with words and phones, making it much easier to see the correspondence between the sounds and the phones that they represent. As can be seen, all of the vowels are characterised by strong formants. Fricatives such as the s in "See" and th in "three", on the other hand, are characterised by broad high-frequency sound and no formants. Stops such as the t in "table" are characterised by silence followed by a burst of high-frequency energy.

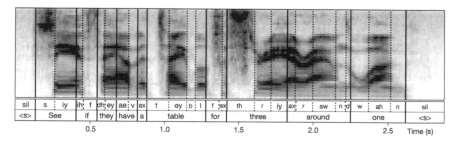

Figure 5.5 *Spectrogram of the sentence "See if they have a table for three around one" annotated with words and phones.*

5.3   Why Is Speech Recognition So Hard?

Whilst the speech signal, as exemplified by the spectrogram, carries most of the information needed to convey the speaker's intention, it is highly variable, often noisy and sometimes incomplete. There are several reasons for this.

Firstly, when a human is speaking normally, inertia prevents the articulators from moving fast enough to fully articulate each sound.

So, very often, even before the articulators reach the target position for the current sound, the brain is sending out signals for the articulators to move to the next sound. This results in a phenomena called *co-articulation*. It means that the actual spectral pattern corresponding to each phone is highly dependent on its neighbours. As a consequence, when I listen to a segment of speech corresponding to a particular phone, I cannot always identify it in isolation.

The second problem I have to overcome is that all humans pronounce words differently due to such things as physiological differences and regional accents. Even the speech of a single speaker will vary depending on their mood, speaking rate and environment. As with co-articulation effects, this variability makes it very difficult to uniquely identify each sound independently of the context. On top of this, as we have seen already, speech is often produced in a variety of background noise conditions such as in a car, adding further variability to the signal.

Thirdly, fluent speech is a continuously varying signal. As explained earlier, when you speak, your articulators are in constant motion, moving from one sound to the next, with the result that there are no cues in the acoustic signal as to where one word ends and another starts. You can see that, in Fig. 5.5, it is impossible to determine from the spectral information exactly where the word boundaries are. If I knew where the words were in the signal, I could train a neural network to decide what each word was, in the same way that I learned to recognise barcodes or hand-written digits. But I can't do this because I don't know where to look.

So speech recognition is hard because the speech signal itself is often poorly articulated and frequently degraded by background noise. Hence, the acoustics alone are insufficient to accurately recognise speech. Humans are able to overcome this and recognise speech effortlessly because they share a common vocabulary and a common understanding of how words are pronounced and how words are combined to form meaningful sentences. This allows them to listen to the speech and find an interpretation which is both consistent with the acoustics and also makes sense linguistically and contextually.

I try to do the same. My neural circuitry is designed to convert the continuous sequence of phones encoded in the spectrogram into the sequence of letters and words that constitute the intended utterance, and in doing this I try to take account of the ways in which words are pronounced and spelt, and how words are strung together to form sentences. However, before I get to that, there are a few steps that I need to take before I can start recognising Steve's speech.

5.4   Capturing the Audio

In order to recognise Steve's speech, I have to route the audio from my microphone to my spectral analyser and then route the stream of spectral speech vectors to my speech recogniser. To ensure that I only recognise words intended for me, I do not start processing audio input until I hear the wake-up phrase "Hey Cyba" and I have verified that the speaker is Steve. Compared with recognising what Steve has actually said, these are relatively straightforward tasks, so they will serve as a good introduction to processing speech with neural networks.

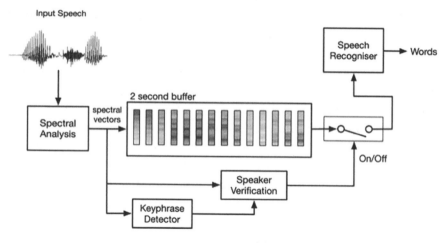

Figure 5.6 *Audio input processing.*

An overview of my audio input processing is shown in Fig. 5.6. Input audio is continuously converted to a sequence of spectral vectors at a rate of 100 per second. Each vector contains 40 intensity values ranging from 100 Hz to 8,000 Hz.[4] These are stored in a buffer which can hold a maximum of 2 seconds' worth of audio, which is ample time to say "Hey Cyba". When the buffer is full, the oldest vectors are overwritten so the buffer always holds the most recent 2 seconds.

When I am waiting for Steve to speak to me, the same vector sequence input to the buffer is simultaneously input to a wake-up phrase detector trained to recognise the phrase "Hey Cyba" and a speaker verifier trained to confirm that the speaker is Steve. If the wake-up phrase detector triggers, it enables the speaker verifier and if the speaker verifier confirms that it is Steve's voice, the buffered stream of spectral vectors is allowed to pass to my speech recogniser. At this point, my speech recogniser starts recognising everything that it hears, including the buffered wake-up phrase. If the first two words recognised are not "Hey Cyba", a false alarm is assumed, in which case the audio stream is switched off, any recognised words are discarded and the wake-up phrase detector is restarted.

Normally, however, "Hey Cyba" is confirmed, in which case recognition continues until silence is detected, marking the end of Steve's utterance. The recognised words are then transferred to the spoken language understanding component and the recogniser restarts. This continues until the end of the conversation is detected, which is indicated by prolonged silence and my conversation manager confirming that it is not expecting Steve to speak again. At this point the audio feed to my speech recogniser is turned off and my wake-up phrase detector is re-enabled. All of this processing ensures that I process only audio which is spoken by Steve and which is intended for me.

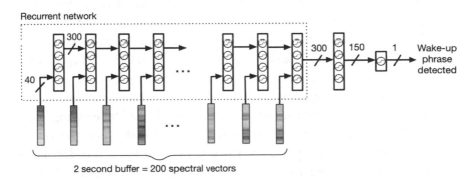

Figure 5.7 *Wake-up phrase detector.*

I outline the structure of the wake-up phrase detector in Fig. 5.7. It is similar to the sequential barcode recogniser that I showed you in

Chapter 3 (see Fig. 3.18). It consists of a recurrent network with a final hidden state connected to a feed-forward network. The main difference is that the input is a sequence of spectral vectors of dimension 40 and there are 300 recurrent neurons in the hidden state. The final hidden state is connected to a two-layer feed-forward network with 150 neurons in the input layer and a single neuron in the output layer, which indicates the probability of the current 2 second sequence containing the wake-up phrase. When this probability exceeds 0.5 for more than five successive time slices, the detector triggers.[5]

The wake-up phrase detector is trained using a few thousand examples of the phrase "Hey Cyba", for which the training target was 1, and around five times as many randomly selected speech segments which do not contain the wake-up phrase, for which the training target was 0. In operation, the detector is very efficient. Every 10 milliseconds a new speech vector is input, the hidden state is updated and the feed-forward network output is recalculated.

My speaker verifier uses another recurrent network to convert the sequence of spectral vectors corresponding to the wake-up phrase into an embedding in exactly the same way as my wake-up detector. However, rather than passing the final state of the recurrent network to a single-neuron detector, I pass the final state to a layer of linear neurons which outputs a vector. The network is trained so that this vector is unique for each speaker. Two of these *speaker vectors* can then be compared using the dot-product operation. If the two vectors are from the same speaker the dot-product will be close to 1, otherwise it will be close to 0.

The way that I use my speaker verifier is shown in Fig. 5.8. I check that the current speaker is really Steve by computing a speaker vector from the wake-up phrase and comparing it with a reference speaker vector precomputed in an enrolment phase from examples of Steve saying "Hey Cyba". To increase robustness, the reference vector is averaged over N examples. This form of speaker verification is said to be *text-dependent* because the phrase to be used for verifying the speaker is fixed in advance, i.e. "Hey Cyba".

The key to maintaining high verification accuracy is to train the network to distinguish between different speakers.[6] This is done by

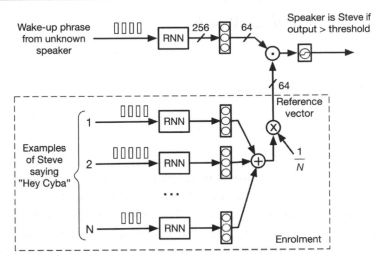

Figure 5.8 *Text-dependent speaker verification. The same recurrent network (RNN) is used to process both the unknown speech and the reference speech.*

collecting a training corpus of speakers each providing multiple renditions of the wake-up phrase. Training then proceeds by repeatedly choosing a random sample of N utterances from one speaker plus a further utterance randomly sampled from either the same speaker or one of the other speakers. These $N + 1$ utterances are input as unknown speaker and enrolment phrases to the set-up shown in Fig. 5.8, with a target output of 1 if the unknown speaker phrase was from the same speaker and 0 otherwise. Once the network is reasonably well trained, the random sampling of other speakers from the training data is modified to favour those whose speaker vectors are close to the enrolment speaker. This improves the ability of the model to discriminate between speakers with similar vocal characteristics. Once the verification network has been trained, the balance between false rejects, i.e. incorrectly rejecting Steve's voice, and false accepts, i.e. incorrectly allowing an imposter to proceed, is determined by adjusting an acceptance threshold. I have this set so that the two types of error are approximately equal. Finally, Steve's enrolment phrases are processed using the trained network and his speaker vector is stored for operational use.

5.5   *From Sounds to Words*

Hey Cyba!
Hi Steve, what can I do for you?
Play some Bach.
Ok, playing Bach's Fugue in D Minor.

Steve wants to listen to some music. There should be just enough time for him to listen to this before he arrives at Hatton Garden.

The core neural network circuitry that I use for speech recognition is called an *encoder–decoder* model (also known as a *sequence-to-sequence model*). As I have previously explained, the hidden state of a recurrent network provides a fixed-length encoding of a sequence of input vectors. We have just seen an example of this with my wake-up detector, where the final hidden state was input directly to the output detector as a representation of the entire sequence of input speech vectors. This type of encoding is an example of an *embedding*. Embeddings are extremely useful because they enable sequences to be converted to a fixed size and then processed in any way I like without having to worry about how long they are. When a recurrent network is used to produce an embedding, it is called an *encoder*.

The process can also be reversed. A fixed-size vector can be used to initialise the hidden state of a recurrent network and then it can be allowed to "free run" by using the output at one time step as the input to the following time step. When a recurrent network is used in this way it is called a *decoder*. Combining an encoder designed to process one type of sequence with a decoder designed to generate a different type of sequence gives me a very useful tool for translating one sequence into another. In particular, I can use it to convert a sequence of spectral speech vectors into a sequence of letters and words.

I will use Steve's music request to illustrate how the encoder–decoder at the core of my speech recogniser works. Figure 5.9 shows the processing, in slightly simplified form, of Steve saying "Play some Bach."[7] The input sequence of spectral vectors are encoded by a recurrent network as shown in unfolded form in the lower half of Fig. 5.9. This network consists

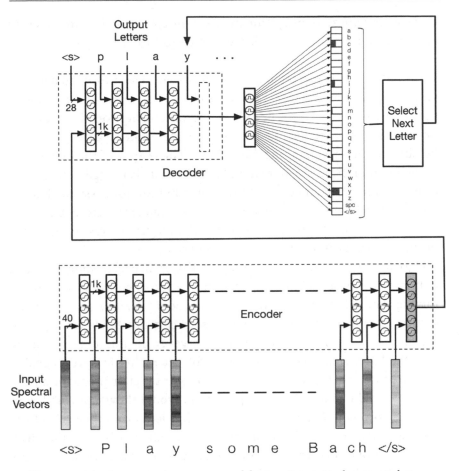

Figure 5.9 *A basic sequence-to-sequence model converting spectral vectors to letters.*

of 1,000 neurons and each neuron receives as input a weighted sum of the current 40-element spectral vector and the 1,000 network outputs from the previous time slot. By the time that the end of the utterance is reached, the 1,000 recurrent network outputs provide a compact encoding, i.e. an embedding of what has just been said (shown in grey in Fig. 5.9).

Having encoded the input speech, the recurrent network decoder then starts to generate an orthographic transcription of the speech letter by letter. The input to the decoder is initially a start of sentence symbol "<s>" and the embedding of the input sequence. Letters are represented by numbers (a = 1, b = 2, etc.) and encoded using a vector in which all the elements are zero except for the element corresponding to the letter (e.g. a would be [1,0,0,0,0,0, …], b would be [0,1,0,0,0,0, …], etc.). This is called a 1-hot representation.

The output of the recurrent network feeds into a feed-forward network which has one output for each possible letter, space or the end-of-utterance marker "</s>". The job of the output network is to predict the next letter based on the current decoder state. Figure 5.9 shows the situation after generating "<s> P l a". The output of the network is predicting that the next letter should be "y" but it also suggests that "i" or "c" is possible. I will come back to this later, but for now, assume that the most likely next letter is always chosen. The sampler therefore selects "y" and feeds it back into the decoder network and the process repeats until the end of utterance symbol "</s>" is generated.

The complete encoder–decoder network is trained by feeding in speech with known transcriptions. Suppose that "Play some Bach" was in the training data. First the spectral vector sequence for this speech would be encoded and then the decoder would start to generate a letter sequence just as it does in recognition mode. However, in this case we know what the letter sequence should be, so for each letter an error signal is calculated and back-propagated from the output letter predictor all the way back to the input. The ideal prediction would show a probability of 1 for the correct letter, and 0 for all the other letters; and the size of the error depends on how different the actual prediction is from the ideal. The back-propagated errors are accumulated and the network weights adjusted to reduce the error. When this is repeated for the entire training set, which in my case consists of around 10,000 hours of speech, the model eventually learns to recognise speech with reasonable accuracy.

During the early stages of training the network's letter predictions are very poor. So, rather than feeding back the most probable letter into the decoder network as is done in recognition, the actual letter from the transcription is fed back. This is referred to as *teacher* training. As recognition improves, the feedback is replaced by the predicted letter so that it can learn to be robust to occasional prediction errors.

In practice, things are a little more complicated than shown in Fig. 5.9. For example, the encoder in my actual speech recogniser uses a bi-directional recurrent network in order to be able to model both previous and future contexts. It consists of two recurrent networks.

One network operates as normal and the second operates on the input sequence in reverse order. The hidden states corresponding to each input vector are then combined. I will show you an example of a bi-directional recurrent network in the next chapter.

The encoder also has multiple layers arranged so that adjacent hidden states are merged at each layer, thereby halving the number of encoder steps at each level. This reduces the length of the input sequence, making it comparable to the rate at which output letters are generated. The decoder also has multiple layers and the set of symbols that it predicts is extended to include frequent clusters of letters such as 'str', 're', 'ing', etc.

In addition to these, there are two further complications which I need to explain in more detail because they are critical not only to the operation of my speech recogniser, but also to many other parts of my neural processing.

5.6 Pay Attention!

Although in principle the final state of a recurrent network can encode all of the relevant properties of an arbitrarily long sequence, in practice memory of the initial spectral vectors is forgotten by the time that last spectral vector is processed. Similarly, whilst in principle a decoder can remember the input from the encoder no matter how many output symbols it generates, in practice it starts to forget the input after a few symbols have been generated.

The solution to this problem is to provide the decoder with an input from the encoder at every prediction step, and to focus the source of this input on the speech corresponding to the letter about to be predicted. This vector is called a *context vector* and it is a weighted sum of all of the encoder states. When the decoder first starts, all of the weight is on the first few encoder states. As the recognition proceeds, the weight moves over the sequence of encoder states, focusing attention on the states corresponding to the currently generated output symbols. These weights are referred to as *attention weights*.

As I mentioned earlier, it is very hard to identify the location of phones or words in speech simply by looking at the spectrogram, so computing the attention weights is not straightforward. As with many hard problems, the solution is to train a neural network to estimate the

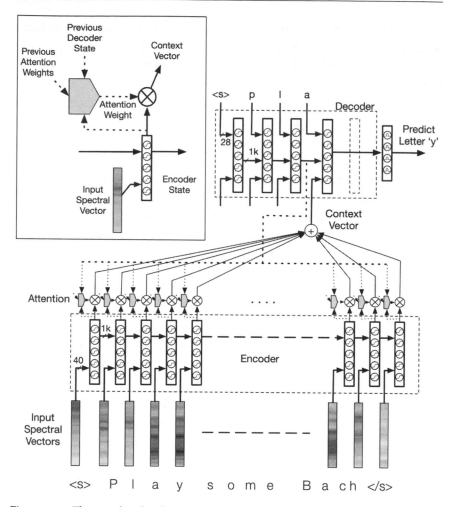

Figure 5.10 *The encoder–decoder speech recogniser shown in Fig. 5.9 extended with an attention layer.*

relevance of each encoder state with respect to the current decoder state. The output of this network provides the *attention weight* required to scale the associated encoder state vector. Adding all of these scaled vectors together then provides the context vector for input to the decoder.

Figure 5.10 illustrates how the basic sound-to-letter recogniser shown in Fig. 5.9 is enhanced by incorporating this attention mechanism, and the inset in Fig. 5.10 shows the processing of just one of the encoder states expanded for clarity. The controlling attention signals are shown by the dotted lines.

You can see that the output of each encoder state is input to the attention network along with the previous decoder state. If the attention network recognises a correlation between these two inputs, the output weight is high and that encoder state plays a strong role in determining the next decoder state. If there is no correlation, the output weight is close to zero and that encoder state is essentially ignored. This is called *content-based* attention because the focus of the attention is determined by the content of the decoder output.

There is, however, an obvious problem with content-based attention in that if an input sound is repeated then the decoder may pay attention to the wrong section of the input. To prevent this, the attention network has a third input, which is the set of attention weights from the previous output step. Access to these weights allows the network to ensure that the mass of the attention weight on the encoder states moves forward monotonically as the decoder generates the corresponding transcription. This latter form of attention is called *location-sensitive* attention.[8]

I can show you how this works for the sentence "Play some Bach" by plotting the attention weights for every output letter. Have a look at Fig. 5.11. Each horizontal row corresponds to the next output letter prediction and each vertical column corresponds to an input spectral vector. You can see the way in which attention focusses on the relevant part of the speech signal as each successive letter is decoded.

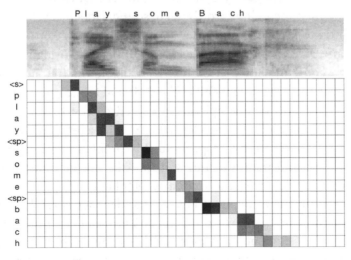

Figure 5.11 *The evolution of attention weights whilst recognising "Play some Bach."*

The use of attention not only improves the accuracy of my speech recognition, but also allows me to process long passages of speech without forgetting what was said to me. Indeed, attention is a generally useful addition to virtually all sequence modelling problems, and we will see more examples of its use as we journey through my inner workings.

5.7   Adding a Language Model

The second complication I need to tell you about concerns the decoder. As shown in Fig. 5.9, the decoder repeatedly predicts the next letter based on the encoded speech signal (focussed by attention) and the sequence of letters already output. It's important to understand that when the encoder–decoder is trained, it is actually trying to absorb three types of knowledge. Firstly, it must learn the correlation between the acoustic signal represented by the spectral vectors and the corresponding letters of the written form. Secondly, it must learn which sequences of letters form valid words; and thirdly, it must learn which sequences of words form valid sentences in the language.

This is a lot to ask! The 10,000 hours of speech used to train my recogniser is equivalent to 3.6 billion spectral vectors, and the transcriptions contain around 100 million words, which equates to about 500 million letters. Now that is a lot of letters and even more spectral vectors, so the model can do a pretty good job of learning the acoustics and how to spell. However, whilst 100 million words might sound a lot, in fact, it is nowhere near enough to learn all the nuances of natural language.

The transcribed speech that I need to train the core recogniser is quite difficult to come by, but written text is available for free in very large quantities; indeed, the web is full of the stuff and text corpora of a billion words or more are commonplace. So I need a way to use all of this written text to augment the encoder–decoder with a better understanding of language. There are two aspects to this problem: first representing the knowledge and then integrating it into the encoder–decoder-based recogniser. Let's deal with the second problem first.

As we saw in the example of Fig. 5.9, the decoder is rarely certain of its prediction of the next letter. Indeed, sometimes the correct sequence of words is not evident until most of the sentence has been spoken, since, for any given phone sequence, there can be multiple possible

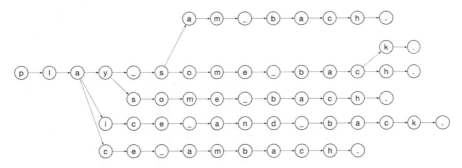

Figure 5.12 *Generating multiple hypotheses from the decoder.*

word sequences. For example, "Play some Bach" could also be "Place Ambach", "Playsome Bach", etc. Some of these word sequences may be genuine possibilities. For example, if Steve was driving north from Munich then he might well have said "Place Ambach" as a rather terse instruction to set the satnav with directions to Ambach!

In order to be able to consider these alternative interpretations of the input speech, the decoder generates multiple alternative hypotheses. Instead of always selecting the most likely letter at each turn, the top few most likely letters are selected to create a branching tree of possibilities as illustrated in Fig. 5.12. If every alternative was retained at every decoding step, the tree would rapidly become unmanageably large. To avoid this, every path through the tree has a score and, when the total number of paths reaches some upper limit, the poorest scoring paths are pruned from the tree. This is called a *beam search* because instead of searching all possible paths, only a beam of the most likely possible paths is considered.

When all of the speech has been processed, the remaining paths in the beam are sorted and the highest scoring paths are passed to my language understanding circuitry for further processing.

The scoring of each path in the tree depends primarily on the product of each letter probability in the sequence. However, it also provides a way to integrate a separate module called a *language model*, trained purely on text, whose sole function is to provide a probability for any word given its history of previous words. Thus, whenever a word boundary is reached in a path through the tree, the probability of the letter sequence is modified by multiplying by the language model probability. This has the effect of reducing the score of paths with unlikely word sequences.

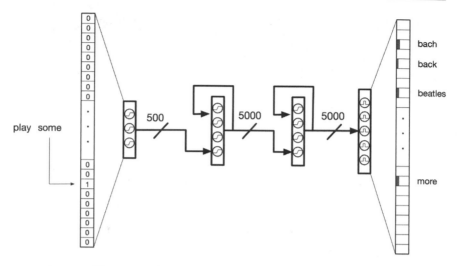

Figure 5.13 *A recurrent neural network language model.*

It probably won't be a surprise to learn that the language model is implemented by using a recurrent neural network.[9] The input is a sequence of 1-hot encoded words and the output is a softmax layer giving the probability of all possible successor words. I have a vocabulary in English of about 100,000 words, so if the 1-hot encoded words were input directly to the language model, there would be an unreasonably large number of weights to train. So instead I use a feed-forward network to embed the 1-hot encoded words into a smaller vector of size 500 and input this to a two-layer recurrent network with a hidden state of size 5,000. The overall architecture of my language model is shown in Fig. 5.13. It is trained on a corpus of text data by feeding in sentences word by word and for each word calculating the error between the 1-hot target defined by the next word in the sentence and the probabilities predicted by the softmax output layer. These errors are back-propagated in the usual way and the parameters updated to reduce the total error.

5.8 A Postscript from the Bard ...

Language models play a crucial role in speech recognition by reducing the possible word sequences to those which are linguistically plausible. It is interesting to note that, just as in the decoder of the speech recogniser, you can use a language model to generate text by sampling the output and feeding it back into the input. As an amusing illustratration of this, I trained a slimmed-down version of my language model on the entire works of William Shakespeare.[10] Here are some randomly generated sentences using this language model:

> *O Lord Archbishop thou hast the world of my sight.*
> *You shall know him by word and for his own shadow*
>   *will I know thee not.*
> *Yet methinks the gods have the Duke of Exeter safe*
>   *that he will come to me.*
> *And methinks thou canst get your worship good Lord Cardinal.*
> *The queen shall see how I did not but what thou wilt*
>   *I had my brother and I am glad*

Although it is nonsense, it is unmistakably Shakespearian in style. Using a language model as a generator is actually useful, and I will return to it when I explain how I construct my responses when I am in conversation with Steve.

Chapter *6*

What Does That Mean?

In this chapter I will explain how I interpret each input utterance and translate it into an equivalent semantic representation. The process of extracting meaning from a sentence is usually referred to as *spoken language understanding (SLU)* and it is one of the most critical components in a conversational agent. Excuse me one moment ...

Hey Cyba, who owns SmartCo?
SmartCo is owned by SmartCo Inc.
Where's it based?
You mean SmartCo Inc?
Yes.
SmartCo Inc is based in Palo Alto.
And the CEO?
The CEO is John Agoulis.
Say again.
The CEO is John Agoulis.
Ok, thanks.

There are many different approaches to SLU and there is little consensus about which is best.[1] Early approaches to the problem used an *analyse and translate* strategy. First a detailed linguistic analysis of each input utterance would be performed in which each word is assigned a lexical role and then grouped into phrases to form a tree-like structure spanning the complete utterance. This structure would then be converted into a general semantic representation such as first-order logic, which is a formal system used in mathematics for symbolic reasoning.[2] Unfortunately, such systems proved to be quite brittle. Natural language is often ill-formed and inherently ambiguous. In the exchange with Steve, it's not clear what "it" refers to in "Where's it based?" and the question "And the CEO?" means little without the preceding context. I also have to deal with speech recognition errors which make these problems worse. Equally problematic is the fact that there are many different ways of encoding information in a knowledge graph and queries often fail because of a mismatch between the semantic encoding of the spoken input and the actual organisation of the data in the graph. In particular, mapping from varied and rich natural language expressions into the correct knowledge graph relations is extremely difficult.

Because I use the representation of a knowledge graph to provide a uniform interface to all of my stored knowledge and to access all of my devices and services, I make the pragmatic choice of using intent graphs to represent the semantics of each input utterance. In order to ensure consistency between the intent graphs output by the SLU and the knowledge graph itself, I use a *generate and rank* strategy in place of the traditional analyse and translate approach. This strategy involves generating candidate intent graphs using the knowledge graph itself as a template and then ranking them to find those which best represent the input utterance.[3] The advantage of this approach is that it guarantees that any intent graph selected to represent the input will be compatible with the knowledge graph. It does, however, mean that I can only understand utterances that refer to things that I already know about. I will explain this strategy first and then describe the neural circuitry that I use to implement it.

6.1   Intent Graph Generation and Ranking

An overview of my intent graph generation and ranking process is shown in Fig. 6.1. The primary input is the utterance to be interpreted, which in the figure is the question "What city does Bill Philips work in?" However, in conversation the interpretation of each input often depends on what has already been said. For example, when I asked Steve "You mean SmartCo Inc?," he replied "Yes", which can only be understood as the answer to a question. To assist handling cases such as these, my conversation manager (described in Chapter 7) provides a context vector which encodes the question just asked and the expected type of the response. This context information is also important when I receive descriptive information from Steve that should be copied verbatim. For example, earlier today Steve asked me to send some flowers. When I asked him "Is there a message?," he responded with "Happy Birthday from Steve." This response provides a value for the *message* property of a *FlowerDeliveryRequest* and I certainly should not attempt to generate an intent graph to represent its meaning!

As I show in Fig. 6.1, there are three main stages to the understanding process. Firstly, I generate a set of candidates, then I fill in any property values[4] and finally I rank the candidates.

In order to generate candidate intent graphs, I must first identify the intent in terms of the action to perform and the *focus* of that action. For example, "What city does Bill Philips work in?" has the intent *Find(Place)* and "Ask Geena to meet me at 3.15 pm." has the intent *Create(Meeting)*.

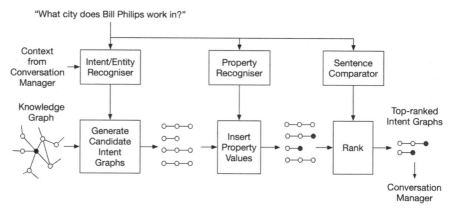

Figure 6.1 *Overview of the spoken language understanding system.*

As well as identifying the intent, I also need to identify any references to *named entities* in the input. *Named entities* are proper nouns such as people, places and organisations which refer to specific unique instances in my knowledge graph. For example, "What city does Bill Philips work in?" contains the named entity "Bill Philips" and "Ask Geena to meet me at 3.15 pm." contains the named entity "Geena". These named entity references must then be linked to the corresponding entities in the graph. Since the verbal reference to a named entity is often imprecise, this is an uncertain process. I try to quantify this uncertainty, by assigning an *entity link score* to each potential match. For example, there are two "Bill Philips" in my knowledge graph. The first is Steve's colleague at SmartCo. The second is an author, and although his name is spelt slightly differently I cannot rule him out since the pronunciation is identical. Of these two matches, the first match to "Bill Philips" receives a higher entity link score because it has been mentioned recently.

The linked entities provide *anchor points* in the graph for finding candidate intent graphs. Starting from these anchor points, I search outwards and generate all possible paths by following the relations in the graph up to a maximum of three hops. Each entity encountered in the graph is replaced by a variable of the same type. This results in a set of candidate intent graphs, typically a few hundred in number. Figure 6.2 shows a selection of the candidates anchored to "Bill Philips" and "Bill

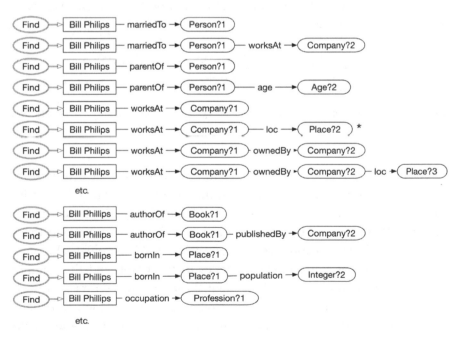

Figure 6.2 *A selection of the candidate intent graphs for the utterance "What city does Bill Philips work in?"*

Phillips", where the correct candidate is starred (since *City* is a kind of *Place*, the starred candidate is equivalent to the intent graph in Fig. 4.5).

The second stage of the process involves recognising property values such as times and places in the utterance and copying them into the corresponding graph nodes. In this example, there are none, but I will come back to this later when I show you a *Create* example.

The third stage of the process is focussed on ranking the candidates to find the intent graphs which most closely match the input utterance. To get a measure of how well each intent graph matches the overall structure of the input utterance, I convert each candidate into an orthographic form based on the relation names and node types. I then compare each candidate with the input utterance using a *comparator network* whose output score is trained to measure the similarity between its two inputs. In both the utterance and the candidate intent graph, named entities are replaced by their types so that the comparison focusses on the overall structure and not the named entities. For example, to compare the input utterance with the starred candidate in Fig. 6.3 the string "What city does <Person> work in" would be compared with "<Person> works at <Company> loc <Place>".

Figure 6.3 *The final top-ranked candidate intent graphs for the utterance "What city does Bill Philips work in?"*

At this point, I have accumulated a number of scores: the probabilities of the intent action and focus type, the link score for each matched entity and the comparator score. For each candidate, I also check how many matches there would be in the graph if it was executed. I group these together to form a feature vector for each candidate, and I add some heuristics such as the number of nodes in the graph and the number of words in the utterance. I then input these feature vectors to a feed-forward network, which generates a ranking score for each candidate. Finally, the top-ranking candidates are passed to my conversation manager, provided that their rank score exceeds a minimum threshold. In the example, the scores of only two candidates were above the threshold and they are shown in Fig. 6.3. The first is the correct intent graph and it would return the correct answer "London". The second, lower-scoring alternative would return the incorrect answer "Palo Alto". When the conversation manager receives multiple candidates, it uses the scores and past history to decide whether to assume the top-ranked candidate is correct or ask a clarifying question.

This is a fairly straightforward example and in practice there are quite a few variations. When there is more than one named entity in the input utterance, the entity with the highest link score is used to seed the candidate intent graph generation and the remaining entities are attached as constraints. When processing property values, I also identify possible aggregator functions. Thus, in the example "Who is Bill's eldest son?", the word "eldest" is tagged with the property *argmax* and the corresponding aggregator function gets attached to compatible numeric nodes in the candidate lists.

I also have to handle the single-word and short-phrase responses that typically occur in conversations such as the exchange with Steve about SmartCo. This exchange also provides examples of various additional intent types that I have for representing specific responses such as *Affirm* and *Negate* for answers to yes/no questions, *Repeat* for requests like "Say that again?" and *Bye* for sign-off phrases like "Ok, thanks." It's instructive to go through this conversation in a bit more detail.

The first turn "Who owns SmartCo?" is a simple well-formed sentence which is handled using the generate and rank process that I just described. In the second turn of the conversation, Steve asked "Where's it based?" This sentence contains no named entities, instead it refers to a previously mentioned one using the pronoun "it". As I have already mentioned, I have a conversational memory in my knowledge graph in which I store the turns of recent conversations. I perform pronoun reference resolution by scanning back through my conversational memory to find entities which have a node matching the intent focus within two hops in the knowledge graph. In this case, I recognised the intent as *Find(Place)* and I only had to go back to the previous turn to find two entities with an adjacent *Place* node: *SmartCo* and *SmartCo Inc.* So I used these as anchors, resulting in the two very similar candidates shown in Fig. 6.4. Since they had similar scores, my conversation manager asked a clarifying question before selecting the first one to execute.

Figure 6.4 *The top-ranked candidate intent graphs for the utterance "Where's it based?"*

Some responses have no associated intent graph at all. When Steve responded with "Yes", I recognised the *Affirm* intent and since there were no more words to process I sent this straight to my conversation manager.

The final query from Steve was the rather terse "And the CEO?" This is quite tricky since there is no question word to indicate the type of entity required and there is no named entity to serve as an anchor. "CEO" is a role which may act as a constraint but, since it is not unique, it cannot serve as an anchor. In situations like this, I resort to the simple heuristic of selecting the most recently mentioned named entity and using it as an anchor. This leads to the single candidate shown in Fig. 6.5.

Figure 6.5 *The top-ranked candidate intent graph for the utterance "And the CEO?"*

The final two turns of the conversation are simple graphless intents: "Say again" is recognised as a *Repeat* intent, and "Ok, thanks" as a *Bye* intent.

Not all utterances have named entities that can be used to seed candidate generation. In these cases, I use the types defined by the ontology to guide the candidate generation process and I use the type of the intent focus as the seed. For example, in "What time is my first meeting today?," the intent is *Find(Meeting)* and the focus *Meeting* generates the set of candidates shown in Fig. 6.6, where the correct candidate is starred (cf. Fig. 4.12).

Create intents are also guided by the ontology even when there are named entities in the utterance. For example, I interpret the utterance "Ask Geena to meet me at 3.15 pm." as a *Create(Meeting)* intent and generate a candidate intent graph as shown in Fig. 6.7.

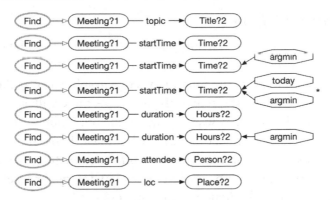

Figure 6.6 *Candidate intent graphs for the utterance "What time is my first meeting today?"*

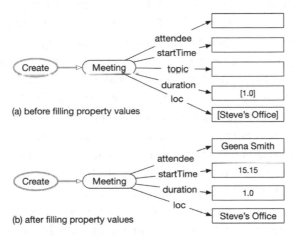

Figure 6.7 *Candidate intent graphs for the utterance "Ask Geena to meet me at 3.15 pm."*

In this case there is only one candidate; however, all property values are empty except for those with specified defaults. In this case, stage two of the generation process is required. The property value recogniser executes and recognises "Geena" as an *attendee* and "3.15 pm" as a *startTime*. These are filled in and the default values are accepted. Any remaining unfilled values, in this case the *topic*, are deleted.

For *Create* intents, the uncertainty is usually not about the structure of the intent; rather it is about the values of the properties. If the property value recogniser is unsure about which property to assign a value to, then I create further candidates to cover the alternative property value assignments.

6.2   *Entity Linking*

As I have explained, the starting point for generating candidate intent graphs is to link each mention of a named entity in the input utterance to the corresponding entity in my knowledge graph. Since spoken references to named entities are frequently imprecise, there will often be more than one possible match, as was the case with "Bill Philips" earlier. Some matches are more likely than others, but I don't just choose the most likely because at this point I don't have enough information. Instead I return all plausible entities along with a match score allowing the final selection to be made later in the candidate ranking process.

I have two conflicting issues to deal with in finding a candidate set of entities. Firstly, I must avoid failing to link an entity because of a minor variation in the way that it was mentioned. Fortunately I don't have to worry about spelling errors because the language model of my speech recogniser only allows words which are in my vocabulary and therefore correctly spelt. However, I do have to be robust to incomplete references and word order variations. For example, if Steve wanted to ask me about his alma mater, he should be able to say "Cambridge", "Cambridge University" or "University of Cambridge". I also have to handle words which are spelt differently but sound the same, since the recogniser may return the same word for both cases. For example, I hear the word "Philips" even if Steve intends "Phillips".[5]

The second issue is that I have several million entities in my knowledge graph and I need to find the correct ones very quickly. I cannot afford to scan through my entire knowledge graph checking each entity in turn to see how well it matches each mention because this would take far too long. I avoid this by building an index. Recall that every entity has a *label* property which defines the official name for that entity. In addition, it may have additional name properties such as *alias, knownAs, givenNames,* etc. (see Fig. 4.3 in Chapter 4 for an example). For every word in my speech recognition vocabulary, I list every entity which has that word in any of its name properties. If any of the entity name properties has a word which is not in my recognition vocabulary then I replace it by the closest-sounding word which is in my vocabulary.[6] For example, both entities *Bill Philips* and *Bill Phillips* get stored under the same word "Philips".

Entity linking is then a two-step process.[7] In the first step, I use the index to retrieve the entities linked to each word of the mention and

I then discard all entities which do not appear in every list. Figure 6.8 shows an example where Steve has asked me "How old is Cambridge University?" The word Cambridge is linked to all entities which have the word Cambridge in their name properties, and similarly the word University is linked to all entities with the word University in their name properties, which includes most of the universities in the world. However, relatively few entities are in both lists: in fact, in my knowledge graph there are only three: Cambridge University, Cambridge University Press, Cambridge University Hospital.

In the second step, I compute a score for each candidate. To do this I assemble a set of features: whether or not the mention is an exact match with the *label* property; the percentage of words in the mention which appear in at least one name property; the number of turns since

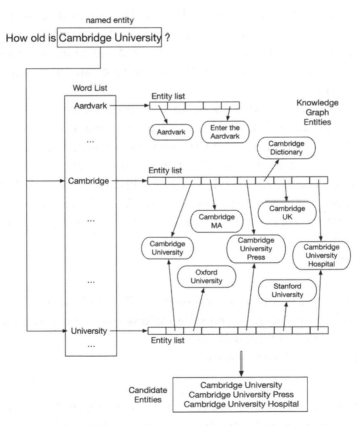

Figure 6.8 *Retrieving candidate entities using the intersection of word-related entity lists.*

the entity was last mentioned; the section of the knowledge graph in which the entity is located; and the percentage character trigram overlap. A character trigram is any sequence of three consecutive letters, and this last measure provides some robustness to changes in endings, for example, inadvertently referring to the "England cricket team" as the "English cricket team". In this case, the trigram overlap is 75% (9/12).

These features are then input to a feed-forward network which has a single output to indicate whether the candidate entity is correct or not. The network is trained on a corpus of dialogues in which the correct entities have been marked for every turn in every dialogue. At each turn, the named entities are extracted, the set of candidate matching entities are retrieved and one incorrect entity is selected at random. Features for both the labelled correct entity and the incorrect entity are computed and input to the network. The error in each case is calculated and back-propagated, and the weights are adjusted. This is repeated until there is no further reduction in the number of errors. In operation, I apply this network to every candidate and discard all entities which score less than 0.5. This typically leaves no more than three candidates to seed the intent graph generation process.

The above process works well for fully specified entities but cannot deal with underspecified mentions such as referring to someone by their first name only. In practice, humans only do this when there is sufficient context to easily disambiguate the underspecified reference. For example, in "Who works at SmartCo and has a wife called Sue?" there are thousands of *Sue*s but only one within a few hops of *SmartCo*, so this is the entity I return, with a score of zero to indicate that its selection is dependent on another entity.

Just a minute . . .

Hi, Steve, this is your 12.15 reminder to call Pedro Navarro.
Ok, call his mobile now and set a walking route to the restaurant.
Walking route to Moulin Rouge set.
Calling Pedro Navarro's mobile.

In addition to the neural network used to score entity matches, the generate and rank strategy that I have just described depends on a variety of other neural networks. Let's have a closer look at how each of these work.

6.3   Multi-task Classification Using a Shared Encoder

Intent recognition, named entity recognition and property recognition all depend on extracting features from the linguistic structure of the input utterance. Whilst the high-level interpretation of these features will be different for each classifier, the lower-level linguistic analysis required in each case will be similar. So, rather than design each classifier separately, they all share a common sentence encoder. The overall structure is shown in Fig. 6.9. Each word in the input sentence is first converted to a word embedding and the sequence of embeddings is input to a recurrent network sentence encoder. The hidden states of the encoder provide the inputs to each of the three classifiers.

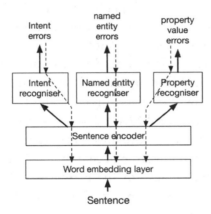

Figure 6.9 *Multi-task classification and training using a shared sentence encoder.*

The great advantage of this arrangement is that I can train all three classifiers simultaneously on the same data. In Fig. 6.9, the dotted lines show the flow of errors during training using error back-propagation. Given a training sentence labelled with named entities, intents and properties, the errors initially pass through their own classifier layers and then they pass into the sentence encoder and finally the word embedding layer. I explained in Chapter 3 that when errors are back-propagated through a network, the same weight will receive multiple corrections, which are added together to determine the actual weight update. The same process applies when the errors originate in different networks.

This *multi-task* training has a number of advantages. Because the sentence encoder receives training signals from different facets of the sentence's interpretation (named entities, intents, properties), it avoids latching on to features which are specific to that particular facet or specific to the particular examples of that facet in the training set. It also prevents a phenomenon called overfitting, whereby a classifier becomes so highly tuned to the training data that, as soon as it is faced with a slightly different example in operational use, it fails. Overall multi-task training results in a more flexible encoder and more robust dependent classifiers.

Multi-task training also provides more efficient use of training data and allows more flexibility in labelling requirements. If one of the facets proves to be difficult to annotate, larger amounts of annotations for the other facets can compensate. Equally importantly, I can pre-train the common encoder substrate as a language model on large amounts of text data in exactly the same way that the language model in my speech recogniser is trained. I connect a feed-forward network with a softmax output layer to the final hidden states of the encoder. I then feed it with text data and train the classifier to predict the next word. When it is fully trained, I discard the feed-forward network. This makes a substantial difference to the eventual performance.[8] Pre-training on large-scale text corpora provides both the word embedding layer and the encoder layer with a generic understanding of the language. Subsequent multi-task training then tunes the embedding and the encoder layers for the specific tasks that I actually require.

Let me now dive into the detail and explain how each of the blocks in Fig. 6.9 actually works.

6.4 Character-Based Word Embedding

The role of the first layer of my multi-task sentence analyser is to convert word symbols to a vector of numbers. In Chapter 5 I explained how I represent words using a simple 1-hot encoding (see Fig. 5.13). This was possible for my language model because my speech recogniser operates with a fixed vocabulary of 100,000 words, and I use the same vocabulary subset for pre-training the encoder. Excuse me again . . .

Hey Cyba, we need help with the dessert menu.
What's a Galette?
Hi Steve, how do you spell that?
G A L E T T E.
It's a crusty tart.
Ok, thanks.

My 100,000 words might seem like quite a lot, but as you have just seen, I sometimes have to ask Steve to spell a word because it is not in my vocabulary. Furthermore, the 1-hot encoding process ignores the semantic similarity between words with similar orthography. For example, as far as a 1-hot encoding is concerned the words "graphical" and "graphics" are no more similar than "graphical" and "pineapple". The output of the embedding network may learn that "graphical" and "graphics" are related because they appear in similar contexts, but it is denied the obvious advantage of being able to see that they are spelt almost the same.

To avoid these problems, my language understanding components use a more sophisticated method for embedding words which is based on the spelling. It is shown in Fig. 6.10. Each character is represented by a 1-hot encoding and then mapped to a fixed embedding using a feed-forward network. These character embeddings are then collected together to form a two-dimensional *embedding matrix* just like the digit images we discussed in Chapter 3. The diagram shows the word "called" being embedded. Each character is converted from a 1-hot vector of size 128 to an embedding of size 16 and, since there are 6 characters in total, the embedding matrix has 16 rows and 6 columns (just 4 rows are shown in the diagram for clarity).

A bank of convolutional neurons then scan the character matrix using a window which has the same height as the character embedding but is narrower. The scan therefore travels from left to right and the resulting feature map is a one-dimensional vector. Each feature map is reduced

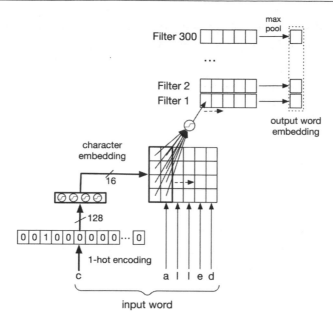

Figure 6.10 *Character to word embedding.*

to a single number by applying a maxpool operation and the output word embedding is then formed by collecting these maxpool outputs to form a vector.

In the diagram, I show all convolutional neurons having a window two characters wide. In practice, I use windows ranging from one to six characters wide to enable the neurons to respond to character sequences of varying length (when the word length is shorter than the window, the neuron just outputs zero). The idea behind this method of word embedding is that the convolutional neurons are able to learn features based on different clusters of letters. As I explained previously, the word embedding layer is pre-trained to act as a language model on general text data and then fine tuned on my annotated task data. This allows the convolutional neurons, to learn features which relate to the role of the word in each sentence and the role of common substrings within related words. In total, I use 300 of these convolutional neurons so the output word embedding is a vector of length 300.

6.5   Sentence Encoding and Recognition

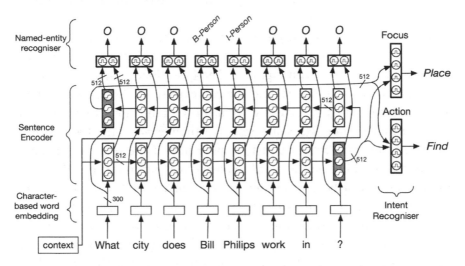

Figure 6.11 *Sentence encoding with intent and named entity classifiers.*

The sentence encoder and the intent and named entity recognisers are shown in unfolded form in Fig. 6.11. The property recogniser is not shown in this diagram, but it is identical in form to the named entity recogniser and I will show an example of using it later.

A bi-directional recurrent network is used for the encoder to ensure each word receives both left and right context. It also reduces the problem of the first word of the sentence being forgotten by the time the end of the sentence is reached. All three recognisers use straightforward feed-forward networks. The intent recogniser connects to the final hidden states of the encoder and the named entity and property recognisers connect to the hidden states corresponding to each word.

Input words are first converted from symbolic form into a fixed-length embedding as just described and then input to the bi-directional recurrent neural network sentence encoder, which is primed with a context vector supplied by the conversation manager. This context vector encodes the dialogue history and the previous question, if any. For the first utterance in the conversation, the context vector is null (all elements are zero).

To illustrate its operation, let's walk through the classification of the sentence "What city does Bill Philips work in?" First I input each word to the character-based encoder, this gives me a sequence of eight word embeddings, each of dimension 300. The word embeddings are then input one by one to the forward recurrent network, which is the lower half of the sentence encoder in Fig. 6.11. The first hidden state is computed from the input word "What" and the context vector. Subsequent hidden states are computed recurrently from the current input word and the previous hidden state. The same process is then repeated for the backward recurrent network, which is in the upper half of the sentence encoder, except that in this case the word sequence is input in reverse. When all hidden states have been computed, the final hidden states (shown in grey in the figure) are input to two feed-forward networks, each with softmax outputs. The first outputs the probability of each possible intent action and the second outputs the probability of each possible focus type. In the diagram, the most likely intent action is *Find* and the most likely focus type is *Place*. If there is significant ambiguity in these classifiers, then I will generate distinct candidates for each possible intent action and focus type.

Named entities can span multiple words, so their recognition is based on a tagging scheme called *IOB tagging*. The first word of a named entity is labelled as *B-T*, meaning *begin* a named entity of type *T*, and any further words are labelled as *I-T*, meaning *inside* a named entity of type *T*. All other words are labelled as *O*.[9] Named entities are detected by finding the most likely IOB tag for each word using a feed-forward network which takes as input the pair of hidden states corresponding to each word. For the example in Fig. 6.11, the first word of the named entity "Bill Philips" is labelled as *B-Person* and the second word is labelled as *I-Person*. All other words are labelled with *O*.

The property recogniser works in exactly the same way except that it tags the input words with properties. For example, Fig. 6.12 shows the processing of the sentence "Ask Geena to meet me at 3.15 pm." In this case, the word "Geena" is labelled with the property *attendee* and "3.15 pm" is labelled with *startTime*. As can be seen, the same IOB labelling scheme is used to identify property values as is used to identify named entities.

From the examples in Fig. 6.11 and Fig. 6.12, it should now be clear what is involved in creating training data for these recognisers. First a

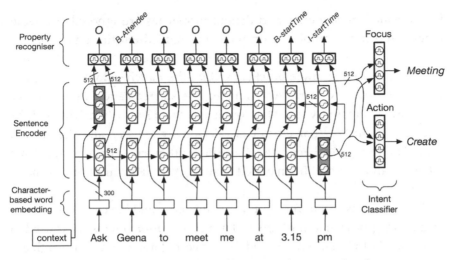

Figure 6.12 *Sentence encoding with intent and property classifiers.*

large set of representative dialogues must be collected. Initially these are sourced from transcriptions of human–human interactions and by setting up so-called Wizard-of-Oz systems in which a human pretends to be an agent and interacts with other humans pretending to be users. Once a system like myself has been deployed, then I can start to collect more realistic operational data, especially for cases where I get things wrong.

In any event, collecting the raw data is relatively easy. The difficult part is annotating the data so that it can be used for training. For this I need the help of human annotators to label each utterance with the intent action and focus, and then label every word belonging to a named entity with the appropriate IOB named entity label, and similarly for every property value, the appropriate IOB property label. This is a non-trivial task and my dependence on large quantities of carefully annotated training data is becoming a major bottleneck to my future development.

6.6   Sentence/Intent Graph Matching

In order to decide which candidate intent graph is the closest match, I convert each candidate to a word string and compare it with the input sentence. Relations and properties with compound names are split into their constituent parts, e.g. *worksAt* becomes "works at" and "startTime" becomes "start time". Where there are branches, each branch is just added in sequence and default properties are ignored. To avoid placing too much emphasis on matching named entities and property values, I also replace every occurrence of a named entity or value with its type enclosed in angle brackets so that the matcher does not confuse it with an ordinary word. As examples, the starred candidate in Fig. 6.2 becomes "<Person> works at <Company> loc <Place>" and this will be matched against "What city does <Person> work in"; and the starred candidate in Fig. 6.7 becomes "<Meeting> attendee <Person> start time <Time>" and this will be matched against "Ask <Person> to meet me at <Time>."

Since the constituent relations in an utterance and the converted intent graph can appear in almost any order, a convolutional network is used to transform both the utterance and the converted intent graph into a fixed-size embedding. The match score is then given by using the dot-product to compute the similarity between the two embeddings.

A diagram of the sentence/intent graph matcher is shown in Fig. 6.13. There are two identical networks, one for the sentence and one for the candidate intent graph. This arrangement is often referred to as a *Siamese network*.[10] For both networks, the input word/symbol sequence is bracketed by start/end symbols and encoded using the same character-based encoder as used in the sentence encoder (Fig. 6.10). These embeddings are then scanned by a convolutional network whose input window is three words wide. The network output vectors are then maxpooled to generate a single embedding representing the whole utterance. This embedding is passed through a single feed-forward network to produce the final vector for computing the similarity score.

The matcher is trained using a mixture of correct and incorrect sentence/intent graph example pairs. Fortunately, there are publicly available datasets consisting of general knowledge questions and the correct answer.[11] I can use this public data to augment my locally collected and annotated data by running my intent generator on each sample question and executing the top few candidate intent graphs. If an intent graph generates the correct answer, I add the sample question plus the intent graph to the set of positive training examples. I also sample an intent graph which generates an incorrect answer and add that to the set of negative examples.

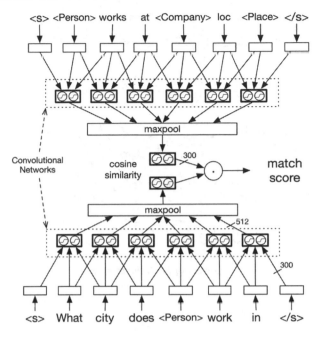

Figure 6.13 *Sentence/intent graph matching using a pair of convolutional networks.*

6.7   Candidate Ranking

In the final processing step, a feature vector is computed for each candidate intent graph. This feature vector consists of the match scores from the initial entity linking, the probabilities of the intent action and focus type and the sentence/intent graph comparator score. To these I add the number of matches there would be in my knowledge graph if the intent were executed, the number of nodes in the intent graph, the number of words in the sentence and the intent itself coded as a 1-hot vector. Each feature vector is then input to a feed-forward network with a single output which is the score for that candidate. The candidates are then arranged in score order.

It would be very hard to train this feed-forward network directly using standard supervised learning because there is no way to label candidates in the training set with the "correct" score. Indeed, there is no correct score. All that matters is that the scores place the candidates in the correct order. So, rather than training the network by minimising the

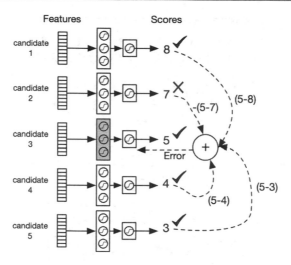

Figure 6.14 *Learning to rank.*

error between the score output and a target, a different strategy called *Learning to Rank* is used.[12]

The neural network ranker is trained using a set of candidates for which the correct pairwise order is known, i.e., for any pair of candidates, it is known which of the pair should be ranked higher. These rankings were produced by human annotators who were given a sentence and two possible candidates from the candidate pool for that sentence and asked to choose the best one.

The basic idea of learning to rank is illustrated in Fig. 6.14, which shows five candidates ranked according to the scores generated by the current state of the ranker. Each candidate is considered in turn and an error correction calculated for it. All of these errors are summed, suitably scaled and then back-propagated through the network. The figure shows the calculation of the error correction for candidate 3 (shown in grey) by summing the differences between its score and all the others. If the ranking was correct, then all of the candidates above candidate 3 would generate negative error corrections, encouraging the neural network ranker to reduce its score for candidate 3, and all of the candidates below candidate 3 would produce positive corrections, encouraging the neural network ranker to increase its score for candidate 3. Thus, if the rank order is correct, the only effect of further training iterations would be to spread out the scores.

However, if the training annotation indicates that a candidate is in the wrong order relative to candidate 3, then the difference is inverted. Thus, in the illustration, candidate 2 should not be above candidate 3 and hence the correction is positive, tending to increase the score for candidate 3 and decrease the score for candidate 2. After each iteration over all of the training data, the ordering implied by the scores will improve until eventually the number of out-of-order pairs is minimised.

I have now explained in some detail how I can listen to an utterance, convert it into words and then into an intent graph. Sometimes a single utterance is sufficient for Steve to convey his requirements and for me to complete the task, but more often each utterance is part of a wider conversation. So the next stop is my conversation manager, to find out how I deal with the problem of deciding what to say next.

Chapter 7

What Should I Say Next?

You have by now seen a variety of exchanges with Steve. These involved straightforward requests such as "Play some Bach." or "What's the time?" These short interactions consisting of a single turn are essentially voice commands. In these cases, my understanding component usually returns a single intent graph which is complete and ready to execute. However, not all interactions are so simple. When Steve asked me to organise a meeting with Geena, I could see from the definition of the *Meeting* type in the ontology that meetings need a topic and I couldn't find one in his request. So I had to ask him to provide one. In that case, the interaction changed from being a command to a *conversation*.

One minute ...

Hey Cyba.
Hi Steve, how can I help?
Send a message to Krissa Maru.
Is that Krissa Maru from the legal department?
Yes.
What's the message?
SmartCo are interested in our proposal.
To Krissa Maru "SmartCo are interested in our proposal," Ok?
Yes, send it.
Ok, its gone.

This exchange illustrates another reason why conversation is often needed. My speech recogniser was not sure whether Steve said "Krissa Maru" or "Chris Amero", both of whom are in his contact list. So Steve's intent was ambiguous. I resolved this ambiguity by selecting the option with the highest confidence but then explicitly asking for confirmation before proceeding.

Conversation enables my interactions with Steve to be much more productive because it allows us to work together to gather all of the required information, resolve any ambiguities and efficiently complete his goals. The way that I think about this is to assume that when Steve speaks to me, he has a goal in mind and my job is to figure out what that goal is and how to fulfil it. Orchestrating this process is the responsibility of my conversation manager.

7.1   My Conversation Manager

I show a high-level view of my conversation manager in Fig. 7.1. Each turn I pass it the intent (or intents if there are alternatives) generated by my SLU, and it generates another intent representing my response. These output intents are the exact analogue of the input intents and they share a similar structure. To avoid confusion, I will follow convention and refer to input intents as *user intents* and output intents as *system intents*. Steve is the user and I am the system!

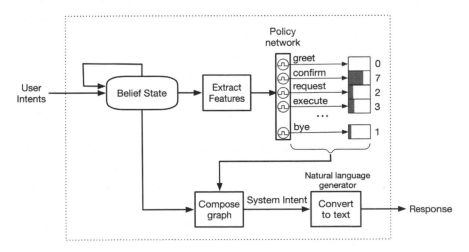

Figure 7.1 *Conversation manager (CM).*

Internally, the conversation manager has three principal components: a *belief state* which represents my current understanding of Steve's goal, a *policy network* which is trained to decide which kind of system intent to execute next given the current belief state and a *natural language generator* which converts the generated system intent into a natural language response.[1]

At the start of the conversation, the belief state is empty. At each turn of the conversation, the belief state is updated with the information in the current user intents. On the first turn, this involves creating goals corresponding to each distinct intent represented in the input. On subsequent turns, the existing goals are augmented or modified to reflect the latest input. Each incoming intent has an associated confidence score computed by combining the confidence scores of the speech recogniser and the SLU components. These scores are carried over so that alternatives in the belief state can also be ranked.

I then extract features related to the current level of uncertainty from the updated belief state. These features include the current turn number, the top-ranked intent type, the confidences of the top-ranked goal, the difference between the top-ranked and second-ranked goal, the number of properties with alternative values, the number of distinct intents, the previous system intent and the number of missing values if the top-ranked goal is a create goal or the number of knowledge graph matches if it is a search goal. This feature vector is input to the policy network, which is a feed-forward network trained to output a score for each possible type of system intent. Normally the system intent type with the highest score is chosen, so in the figure the *Confirm* intent would be selected. This choice then conditions a heuristic algorithm which scans the belief state and constructs a system intent graph. For example, when conditioned by the *Confirm* intent, it would search belief state for a branch to confirm which has a plausible alternative.

Let me illustrate how the conversation manager works by stepping through the previous interaction with Steve. Figure 7.2 shows the user intents, the belief state and the selected system intent for each of the five turns of the conversation.

At the first turn, Steve greeted me but gave no further information. At this point, the belief state is empty, so I responded with a *Greet* intent which resulted in a "How can I help you" greeting. Steve then

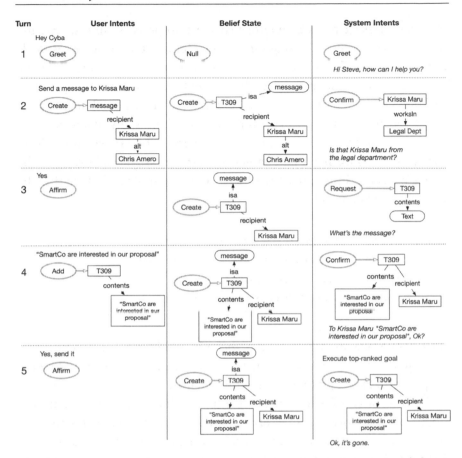

Figure 7.2 *Trace showing the evolution of the belief state during a conversation with the goal of sending a message.*

asked me to send a message to Krissa Maru, which was translated into a *Create(Message)* intent. My speech recogniser thought that the name "Chris Amero" was also a possible, though somewhat less likely, recipient so it was added as an alternative property value using the *alt* relation. A message instance, *T309*, was tentatively created and my policy network selected a *Confirm* system intent. To ensure that the candidate entity *Krissa Maru* was clearly identified, a relation to further describe her was copied from my knowledge graph and added to the *Confirm* system intent, in this case, *worksIn Legal Dept*. In turn 3, Steve confirms the recipient, and my belief state is updated by removing the alternative.

The type *Message* has a mandatory *contents* property, so in response my policy network selected a *Request* system intent. In turn 4, Steve responds and an *Add* intent provides the requested information. Notice that the SLU candidate generator used the context provided by the previous question to provide the message ID and *contents* relation. My belief state is updated and it now appears complete; nevertheless, my policy network decides to confirm that the entire goal is correct before executing it. In turn 5, Steve confirmed that I should send the message, so I executed the *Create(Message)* intent, reset the belief state and informed Steve that the message had been sent.

Hey Cyba, what's Smart car's current price?
Hi Steve, the fortwo electric Smart car costs £18,000.
No, I want SmartCo's share price.
Sorry, SmartCo's share price is $42.7 up 2.1%.

For Krissa Maru and Chris Amero, the only ambiguity was in a property value. In this latest exchange, I misunderstood entirely. You can see what happened in Fig. 7.3. My SLU thought the most likely goal was a request to find the price of a new Smart car, but it did offer a request to find SmartCo's share price as an alternative. When Steve repeated the request, my SLU still thought that he was asking for the price of a Smart car, but this time the belief state update took account of the *Negate* intent and demoted the top-ranked goal so that this time when the policy network decided to execute the top-ranked hypothesis it got the answer Steve wanted.

When I executed the SmartCar price query, additional properties were retrieved from my knowledge graph in addition to the price. When my confidence in the top-ranked hypothesis is not high, additional properties are added to my response in order to make Steve fully aware of the question that I am answering. If I had just answered "£18,000" then Steve would have realised that a share price of £18,000 is unlikely, but he might have put this down to a glitch in the stock-market price service that I use rather than me completely misunderstanding the question.

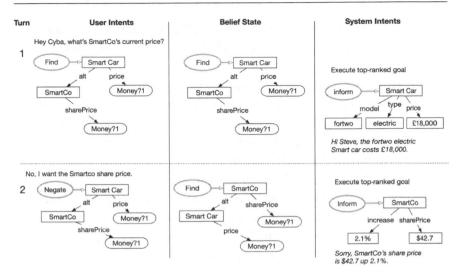

Figure 7.3 *Trace showing the evolution of the belief state through a second conversation.*

7.2   Learning a Good Dialogue Policy

As we have seen, a key decision at each turn in a dialogue is choosing what to do next, and this is not always easy. Suppose that in the earlier conversation the intended recipient was *Krissa Maru* with probability 0.7 and that it was *Chris Amero* with probability 0.3. What should I have done next? My options were to play safe and ask Steve to confirm the recipient or be bold and assume the most likely name was correct and proceed. Adopting an overly prudent strategy could easily irritate Steve since in this case 7 out of every 10 confirmations would be a waste of time. On the other hand, being over-confident runs the risk of making serious mistakes, for example, by sending a message to the wrong person. What makes this problem particularly difficult, and unlike anything I have discussed before, is that the impact of each individual decision depends on how the dialogue evolves in the future and furthermore, the future evolution is dependent on those earlier decisions. In the example, my policy network decided to confirm the entire message contents and recipient before sending it. So taking the bold option earlier on would not have been fatal, but it might nevertheless have taken more effort to recover if the recipient had indeed been *Chris Amero*.

This is a complex optimisation problem. Since I cannot tell in isolation whether each individual decision made by my policy network is correct or incorrect, I cannot train the policy network by learning from examples. Instead the solution to this problem requires *reinforcement learning.*[2]

Here's how this works. Firstly, I need a measure of goodness called a *reward* function in order to rate the quality of each conversation. I apply this reward function at every turn in the conversation, and the total reward over the course of the conversation provides the overall measure of goodness that I would like to maximise.

My reward function is simple but effective. I give each turn a reward of −1 and at the end of the dialogue I give a reward of +10 if I fulfil Steve's goal and −10 if I fail. The final reward therefore strongly encourages success and the per turn penalty encourages me to keep our conversations short and efficient.

At every turn in the dialogue in Fig. 7.1, my policy network outputs a score for each possible system intent and I normally proceed through the dialogue by always choosing the system intent with the highest score. This score is actually an estimate of the future reward that I can expect to receive by choosing a specific system intent and thereafter following the policy (by always choosing the highest-scoring system intent). So, for example, on choosing the *Confirm* intent in Fig. 7.1 I would expect to receive an additional reward of 7 in the future, but if I had chosen the *Request* intent I would expect to receive only 2 in the future.

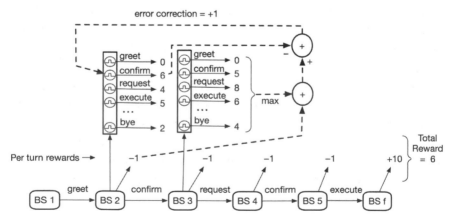

Figure 7.4 *Training my policy network using Q-learning.*

This predictor of future reward is called the *Q-function*, and it provides the key to training my policy network because it provides a very simple rule: given my choice of system intent at the current turn, the Q-function prediction for that choice should equal the actual reward I get at that turn plus the maximum possible Q-function prediction at the following turn. If I train my policy network to adhere to this rule, it will learn the required Q-function. This is illustrated in Fig. 7.4 which shows the situation at turn 2 of the dialogue traced out in Fig. 7.2.

Along the bottom of the figure is shown the sequence of belief states; technically this is referred to as a Markov decision process. The transitions between them are labelled with the selected system intent and the corresponding reward. At turn 2, the policy network predicted a future reward of 6 for taking the *Confirm* intent and received a per turn award of −1. However, the maximum predicted future reward at turn 3 is 8, which is reduced to 7 when the previous per turn award is added. Thus, the estimate for taking the *Confirm* intent at turn 2 was low, and hence an error correction of +1 is applied to the output neuron corresponding to the *Confirm* intent.

By scanning every turn of every conversation and continuously correcting the predictions, the policy network eventually learns to predict the Q-function accurately. This process is called *Q-learning*. What is perhaps surprising is that it not only learns to predict the future reward accurately, but also at the same time learns the best possible policy, the so-called *optimal policy*. This is a result of always correcting the current prediction to be closer to the maximum possible reward at the next turn. Over time, when the prediction at every turn is accurate, always choosing the system intent with the highest score must on average yield the maximum possible total reward.[3]

Q-learning will find the optimal policy only if the training dialogues contain examples of all possible input belief states and all possible transitions. If all of my conversations are guided by my policy network, this won't happen. To learn an optimal policy, I must occasionally try something different. So every so often, rather than choosing the highest-scoring system intent, I choose a system intent at random. In reinforcement learning jargon, this is called *exploring*.

The problem, of course, is that my interactions with Steve are my only source of data, and behaving randomly, even if only occasionally, could be dangerous. For example, randomly executing a send message goal before the contents and recipient had been checked wouldn't go down at all well. Transferring money to the wrong person in a banking transaction would be even worse! In practice, I try to mitigate this problem by restricting exploration to plausible alternatives and avoiding actions which cannot be reversed.

There is a second practical problem. In order to compute my reward function I need to know whether I completed each goal successfully or not and unfortunately this is not always easy to determine. If I sent a message in error or transferred money to the wrong person, Steve would indicate my error immediately both verbally and by trying to undo it. If I play the wrong track, or turn on the wrong light, then Steve would correct the error and again I would know that I had got it wrong. There are cases, however, where Steve just ignores the error or simply doesn't realise that I got it wrong. General knowledge queries typically fall into this category. To mitigate this problem, I only train on conversations where I have some explicit indication of the outcome.

It can take many thousands of conversations to learn an optimal policy. So my policy network was trained initially by interacting with a simulator, which is an agent a bit like me pretending to be Steve.[4] This allowed me to provide a reasonable conversational behaviour from the beginning. Then, once I started interacting with Steve for real, I was able to slowly improve my behaviour in the background without him really noticing.

7.3   Conversational Memory

As I mentioned in the introduction, I record my interactions with Steve in my conversational memory. For each conversation, I store everything that has been *grounded*, that is, all of my system intents and executed goals. The main use of this conversational memory is to allow my SLU components to interpret everything that Steve says to me in context. In particular, it allows me to resolve anaphoric references such as pronouns and underspecified names. For example, this morning when Steve asked me "How long will it take to drive there?," "there" is referring to the place of the meeting, the Hatton Garden office. When later he asked "Do you have their home address?," "their" is referring to Bill and Sue.

The task of relating a pronoun to the entities to which it refers is called *coreference resolution*.[5]

In general, coreference resolution is a difficult task and it requires a detailed understanding of the semantics to get it right. A classic example is the following:

The city council denied the demonstrators a permit because

1. they feared violence.

2. they advocated violence.

In the first ending, "they" refers to the city council, whereas in the second ending, "they" refers to the demonstrators. I gave a similar example in the introduction as an example of natural language understanding that required a precise analysis of the semantics of the utterance and commonsense reasoning. Since both of these are beyond my capabilities, I can do little more than guess in cases like these.

Fortunately, task-oriented dialogue is more straightforward and the referent is usually obvious. My basic algorithm is to look back in time through the system intents and goals in my conversational memory to find the first entity which matches the pronoun in number and gender. This processing takes place in my SLU. The named entity recogniser tags pronouns as entity references and then my entity linker looks for a match in the conversational memory.

7.4 Generating My Response

The final task of the conversation manager is to convert the abstract graph structure that I use internally to represent system intents into natural language. Some of the most common system intents have a specific role in conversations and there really aren't many different ways I can render them. For example, for *Greet* I just choose from a few stock phrases such as "Hello, Steve." or "Hi, Steve, how can I help?"; similarly for *Affirm* I can say "Yes", "That's right" or "Correct" but there aren't many other options.

System intents which carry information generated through interaction with my knowledge graph are more complex. They contain relations and values in many different combinations, and selection from stock phrases or using simple templates is not practical. So for these I use neural circuitry to convert system intent graphs into natural language.

You will remember that in Chapter 5 we had some fun by training a language model on Shakespeare and then using it as a decoder by sampling the output and feeding it back into the input. Although the output was meaningless, it looked distinctly Shakespearian because the recurrent network model had learned the structure and style of Shakespeare's writing by training on his complete works.

By training a recurrent network on a corpus of typical conversational responses, I can do the same thing for my response generator. Except, of course, I need to generate sentences with a specific meaning. To do this, I use an encoder–decoder arrangement in which I first encode the system intent graph and then input the embedding to a recurrent network decoder.[6] To make things a little easier I reduce the training requirements by using a simple trick called *de-lexicalisation* to reduce the working vocabulary. This is illustrated in Fig. 7.5. Each value in the input system intent graph is replaced by a token denoting its type, and the corresponding natural language utterance is generated from this

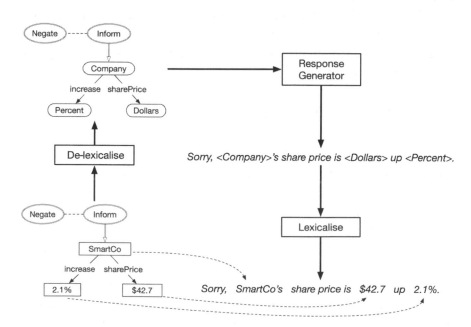

Figure 7.5 *De-lexicalisation and re-lexicalisation.*

de-lexicalised intent. The type tokens in the de-lexicalised output are then replaced by the actual values to produce the final output. In effect, the system becomes a generator of sentence templates into which actual values are slotted to produce the final output.

The encoder–decoder structure that I use in my speech recogniser is a sequence-to-sequence model where the input is a sequence of spectral vectors and the output is a sequence of letters. I also use sequence-to-sequence models to synthesise speech and translate from one language into another and I will tell you about these things in later chapters. For response generation, however, the input is an intent graph, which in general is not a sequence but a tree structure, so a regular recurrent network encoder cannot be used. Instead I use a simple extension called a *tree recurrent neural network (treeRNN)* which allows trees rather than sequences to be encoded.

As I have explained, a recurrent neural network in unfolded form is identical to a standard feed-forward network in which there are as many layers as there are input vectors and in which the weights in each layer are shared. When a sequence is input to a recurrent network, the hidden state is updated for each successive input by taking the weighted sum of the current input vector plus the weighted sum of the previous hidden state. At the end of the sequence, the final hidden state provides an embedding of the entire sequence. A treeRNN is identical except that instead of a linear sequence, the input is a branching tree which starts at the leaf nodes and ends at a single root node.

This is illustrated in Fig. 7.6. On the left is an intent graph consisting of entity and type nodes joined by labelled relations. The first step is to convert the labelled relations to nodes as shown in the centre of the figure. This tree structure is embedded by first creating an unfolded recurrent network with hidden states exactly matching the tree as shown in the centre of the figure. The tree embedding is then generated by inputting the node labels into the tree starting from the leaf nodes and ending at the root. The calculation of each hidden state is identical to a standard recurrent network except that, when two hidden states meet, they are added together.

The way I use this tree encoder to generate natural language responses is shown in Fig. 7.7 partway through generating the response shown in

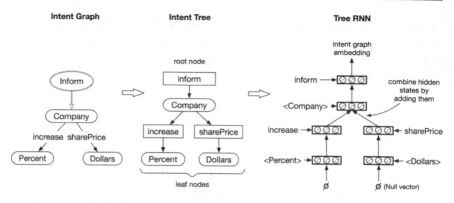

Figure 7.6 *Embedding an intent graph by converting it to a neural tree structure.*

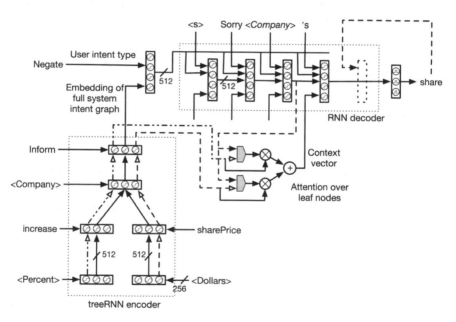

Figure 7.7 *Tree-encoder-based natural language response generator partway through generating "Sorry, SmartCo's share price is $42.7 up 2.1%."*

Fig. 7.5. The recurrent tree encoder is shown in the bottom left of the figure. Ignore the dotted lines for the moment.

At the lowest level of the tree, the types *Percent* and *Dollars* are input. These are place holders for the actual values of 2.1% and $42.7. The hidden states of these leaf nodes are propagated upwards and at the next level the property names *increase* and *sharePrice* are input. Again, the hidden states are propagated upwards, but this time they join a single node so they are added together. This node represents the focus of the system intent, which is the type *Company*, a placeholder for SmartCo. Finally, the hidden state propagates up to the root node which represents the system intent itself, in this case the *Inform* intent. The hidden state output from the root node now represents an embedding of the entire system intent graph. It is joined with the type of the preceding user intent, in this case *Negate*, using a 1-hot representation and input to the decoder.

In addition to its own recurrent state, the decoder takes three inputs at each step of the generation process: the embedded system intent, the previous output token (i.e. word or placeholder type) and a context vector computed by an attention mechanism.

As in my speech recogniser, it is important to focus each step of the generation process on the relevant part of the system intent. In a regular encoder, the attention mechanism scans over the hidden states of the input sequence. In a tree-based encoder, the nearest equivalent would be to scan the leaves of the tree. However, the leaves are dependent on their parents and the representation of each leaf node must take account of the path from that node up to the root. Hence, as well as computing an embedding for the full system intent, the encoder must also compute an embedding for each individual leaf node. It does this by treating the path from leaf to root as a sequence and encoding it as for a regular recurrent network. These sequences are shown by the dashed and dash-dotted lines in Fig. 7.7. The embeddings for each leaf node are then compared with the previous decoder state to generate the attention weights for each leaf. The leaf embeddings are then scaled and summed to provide the context vector for the next step of the decoding process.

The generation process outlined above produces reasonably natural renditions of each input system intent. However, it has a flaw. There is nothing to stop the generator repeating itself and nothing to encourage the generator to avoid omitting important information. Thus, typical outputs for the generator above might be

1. Sorry, SmartCo's share price is $42.7 up 2.1% up 2.1%.
2. Sorry, SmartCo's share price is up 2.1%.
3. SmartCo's share price is $42.7 up 2.1% at $42.7.
4. etc.

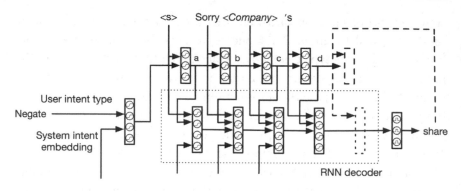

Figure 7.8 *Natural language decoder with output token tracking.*

In order to reduce this effect, I filter the input to the decoder using a second *output token tracking* recurrent network as shown in the modified decoder of Fig. 7.8. I initialise the tracking network with the utterance start symbol "<s>" and the full system intent embedding. At each decoder step, the last token generated is input to the tracking network, enabling it to modify the system intent embedding before the next item of information is rendered. The modified system intent embedding is then input to the decoder for the next generation cycle. During training, the tracking network learns to filter information from the system intent embedding once it has been rendered. This process is illustrated in Fig. 7.9, which shows a stylised depiction of the tracker layer hidden state. Initially it contains all of the information in the system intent embedding.

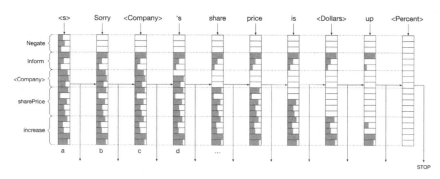

Figure 7.9 *Filtering the system intent to prevent omissions and duplications in rendering. The labels a, b, c, d relate to the generation steps shown in Fig. 7.8.*

As each output word is rendered, the tracker discards the information that is no longer needed and when all of the information has been rendered the tracker hidden state is all zero, marking the end of the utterance.

By filtering the system intent embedding at each step, I prevent the generator from repeating itself, and when all information has been rendered, the empty residual system intent provides a very clear signal that I have reached the end of the utterance. The net effect is to significantly reduce rendering errors.

My neural response generator is trained on examples of system intents and their natural language equivalents in much the same way as all of my other encoder–decoder networks. Each training example is presented to the network and the difference between the predicted output and the actual output is used to compute an error signal which is back-propagated through the network. As with my speech recogniser, the early stages of training use a teacher mode in which actual tokens are fed back to the decoder rather than predicted tokens. As performance improves, the feedback is replaced by the predicted token so that the network can learn to be robust to occasional prediction errors.

As with all supervised training, finding sufficient training data is a challenge, made worse in the case of natural language generation because there are no naturally occurring sources of good-quality data. In the case of spoken language understanding, data from humans interacting with agents can be collected and transcribed. The transcription is certainly costly, but it can be done. However, collecting data from human agents talking to other humans is not helpful because there are no corresponding system intents, and the language used by human agents talking to other humans will be far too wide-ranging. The solution that my developers used was to randomly generate and display system intents in a simplified graphical form along with the dialogue history to human annotators and ask them to say how they would express the displayed concept. With a little training, they became quite good at this task. Nevertheless, as with all supervised training, the limited availability of training data inevitably limits progress. You will have observed that this is becoming a common theme!

Sorry, another interruption …

Hey Cyba, leave him.
I am sorry but I don't understand you.
I didn't speak to you, delete what you heard.
Ok, apologies – memory wiped.

Oh dear, that was a false trigger. I think Steve was saying something like "In case I believe him …" in his meeting with Geena and somewhere in there I wrongly heard the words "Hey, Cyba". Notice that Steve asked me to delete what I overheard from my memory. I will say more about this in Chapter 11 when I talk about trust.

The final step in the conversational cycle is to convert my responses back into speech. This means moving from the digital world of printed words into the analogue world of audio signals using a process called *speech synthesis*. I will discuss this next.

Chapter 8
Listen to Me

The final stage in the pipeline from Steve speaking to me responding is the conversion of the text message generated by my conversation manager into speech. This process is referred to as *text-to-speech synthesis*.

8.1   From Text to Speech

I explained in Chapter 5 that humans produce speech by forcing air from their lungs through the vocal cords and moving their jaw, mouth and tongue to produce a continuously varying acoustic pressure wave. This is a complex biological system and, although there have been many attempts to reproduce its effect digitally, the quality of the synthesised speech is modest and often contains distracting artefacts.[1]

My goal is to sound natural in conversations, not to mimic human speech production. So I ignore the way that humans produce speech and instead focus on how they hear it! As I explained when I was describing my speech recogniser, the human ear behaves like a time-varying spectrum analyser operating on a non-linear frequency scale called the mel-scale. The speech that the ear hears can be visualised as a mel-scale spectrogram as in the example shown in Fig. 5.3. If it were possible to convert text into a mel-spectrogram which was indistinguishable from a mel-spectrogram derived directly from human speech, then the speech reconstructed from that mel-spectrogram should also be indistinguishable from human speech. This motivates my perception-oriented approach to speech synthesis.

Hey Cyba, what's the time now?
It's four pm.

Figure 8.1 provides a high-level view of how I converted the answer to Steve's question into a speech waveform that he could hear. The primary output from my conversation manager is the response in text form, in this case, "It's 4 pm." These responses often include symbols and abbreviations which need to be converted into words before they can be synthesised. The first step in the synthesis is therefore to pass the response through a text processor which identifies each different kind of symbol such as a time, date, email address, etc. and converts it to an appropriate spoken form. In this case, my text processor converts the number 4 to the word "four".

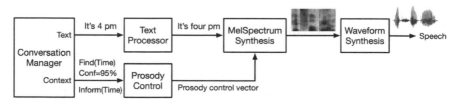

Figure 8.1 *Overview of my text-to-speech synthesis system.*

The next stage of the process is to convert the word sequence into the sequence of mel-spectra which form the mel-spectrogram. This process is the inverse of my speech recogniser and not surprisingly I use an encoder–decoder to implement the transformation. However, the synthesis process requires something extra. When a human speaks, they encode the words as a sequence of sounds but they also encode extra information in the way that they intone the speech in terms of the pitch, intensity and duration of their voice. This extra information can be used to distinguish between a statement and a question, express varying degrees of confidence, surprise, disbelief, and convey emotion such as happiness, sadness, or anger. This sentence-level information is called *prosody* and whilst it is mostly ignored by my speech recogniser, it is important to human perception and cannot be ignored by my synthesiser.

I cannot match the range and subtlety of human prosody, but I do try to distinguish between a question and a statement and ensure that my responses sound appropriate to the context. For example, if my confidence is low, then I try to sound unsure and if I have conflicting information I try to sound confused. Providing this extra control signal into my text-to-mel-spectrum synthesiser is the job of prosody control, which depends on three additional signals from my conversation manager: the type and focus of the user intent, the overall confidence that I have decoded this intent correctly, and the type and focus of the resulting system intent. In the example, I recognised the user intent *Find(Time)* with 95% confidence, and in response generated an *Inform(Time)* system intent. This is a fairly routine response and the generated prosody in this case was neutral.

The final stage of the synthesis process is to convert the sequence of mel-spectra into a speech waveform which can be output to a speaker. To do this I input each mel-spectrum to a neural network generator trained to generate waveforms sample by sample. Since waveforms are highly correlated over quite long periods, I use for this task a special form of convolutional neuron called a *dilated* convolutional neuron which is able to efficiently look back many samples into the past. Excuse me one moment ...

Hey Cyba, any new messages?
Hi Steve, you have two unread messages.
Ok, read them.
First message from Krissa Maru:
"We need to close before year end 2020."
Second message from PA to John Agoulis:
"Can you talk to Dr Agoulis at 1pm PST?"
Ok, set up a call with Dr Agoulis at 9pm UK time.

As well as synthesising the responses generated by my conversation manager, here I also had to synthesise messages written by other humans over which I have no control of the content. This emphasises the need for me to be able to handle any kind of text message, not just my own responses. Let me now explain in more detail how each of the components in Fig. 8.1 works.

8.2 Text Processing

My speech synthesiser must be able to read out arbitrary text messages as well as verbalise the responses generated by my conversation manager. In addition to the words of the language, text messages include a variety of other symbols such as numbers, ordinals, years, dates, money, email addresses, etc.

Each of these so-called *semiotic* classes has its own rules for writing the textual form and verbalising as speech. For example, 2020 is either "two thousand and twenty" or "twenty twenty" depending on whether it is a number or a year. In principle it would be possible for my synthesiser to learn that 2020 is sometimes pronounced "two thousand and twenty" and other times pronounced "twenty twenty", but in practice it would take an exorbitant amount of data. Furthermore, it would be rather pointless since once the semiotic class of a symbol is known, the rules to convert it to words are straightforward to implement.

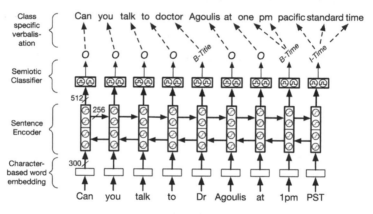

Figure 8.2 *Semiotic processing of text message "Can you talk to Dr Agoulis at 1pm PST?"*

There are also a variety of special-case abbreviations that I need to resolve. In the message from John Agoulis, "Dr" is an abbreviation for "Doctor", but in an address the same abbreviation would denote "Drive". Again, once the semiotic class is known, in this case *title* and not *address*, the expansion from abbreviation to words requires only a simple table lookup.

Hence, I process all incoming text before passing it to my speech synthesiser by tagging the words and symbols with semiotic classes using the same IOB labelling scheme that I use for named entities in my SLU component. The neural network that I use for this is very similar to the one I told you about in Chapter 6. Input words are transformed to 300 dimension vectors using a character-based embedding and then input to a bi-directional recurrent network. The forward and backward hidden states corresponding to each word are combined and input to a feed-forward network trained to distinguish between 14 different semiotic classes.[2]

I illustrate an example of this text processing in Fig. 8.2. Following labelling, any tagged words are processed by class-specific conversion routines. In the example, the *Title* routine converts "Dr" to "doctor" and the *Time* routine converts "1pm PST" to "one pm pacific standard time".

8.3   Neural Speech Synthesis

The core of my neural speech synthesis circuitry is shown in Fig. 8.3 at the point where it has synthesised the first two words of "How may I help?"[3] The text to be synthesised is shown at the bottom of the figure and the partially constructed spectrogram is shown at the top. The overall structure is very similar to my speech recogniser. The input text is first encoded and then a decoder generates the spectrogram slice by slice, just as the recogniser generated the output transcription letter by letter.

The encoder consists of three stages. Firstly, each letter is converted to a character embedding similar to the embedding used in my SLU components shown in Fig. 6.10. Several layers of convolutional neurons are then applied, with character windows ranging from 1 to 7. The aim of this stage is to learn the features needed to pronounce each word based on clusters of characters of varying lengths. The final stage consists of a bi-directional recurrent network which encodes the characters based on their context within the utterance. This is necessary for resolving pronunciation challenges like "Lead me to the lead mine".

Sitting between the encoder and the decoder is an attention layer which works exactly the same as in my speech recogniser. For each cycle of the decoder, the encoder states are scaled by attention weights and then added to form a context vector which is input to the decoder to generate the next slice of the spectrogram. The attention weights are determined by comparing the previously generated spectral slice with the

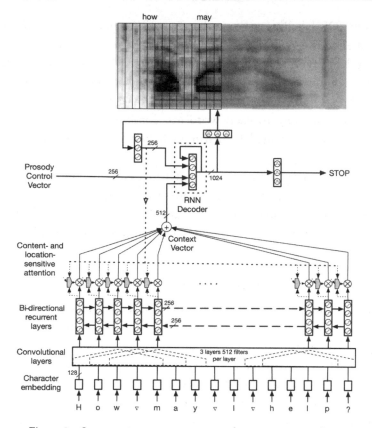

Figure 8.3 *Sequence-to-sequence text to mel-spectrogram synthesis.*

corresponding encoder state conditioned by previous attention weights to ensure that the focus of attention proceeds monotonically over the input letter sequence.

The recurrent network decoder takes as input the current context vector, the prosody control vector and an embedding of the previously generated spectral slice and generates a new spectral slice. It also separately generates a binary stop signal to indicate when the process should terminate.

The sequence-to-sequence model was trained using the voice of a professional human speaker who read my side of a large number of simulated conversations, over 100 hours in total. For each simulated conversation, the text of my response and the context signals from my conversation manager were saved and for each response, a target mel-spectrogram was computed directly from the human speech.

For each turn of every training conversation, the text of my response was input to the synthesiser and an error computed between the predicted mel-spectrogram and the target mel-spectrogram. This error was then back-propagated through the network and the parameters adjusted accordingly. This training also requires an appropriate prosody control vector for each training utterance. This was generated by a *prosody encoder* network which was trained in parallel with the main synthesiser using exactly the same training data, as I will shortly explain.

8.4   Setting the Right Tone

Earlier I explained the importance of prosody in natural conversation. Prosody governs the overall acoustic structure of an utterance above the level of the individual sounds. As well as intonation, prosody includes stress, rhythm, mood and emotion. Just a moment ...

Hey Cyba, order me a pizza.
Ok Steve, what topping would you like?
Er ...
There's ham or chicken ...
I'll take a pepperoni.
Ok, I have ordered it.

Steve must be planning to work late tonight!

This short exchange is a good example of the importance of prosody. When Steve couldn't decide on a topping, I tried to help by suggesting some possibilities such as ham or chicken. My pitch rose on "chicken" to signal that I was suggesting items from a list and these were not the only options. This encouraged Steve to consider something different and indeed he chose pepperoni. If ham or chicken had been the only possibilities, my intonation would have fallen on "chicken" to signal that this was an either–or choice. This would have discouraged Steve from considering something different, which was not my intention.

You can see these effects in the upper part of Fig. 8.4, which shows a spectrogram of the phrase "ham, or chicken" as I spoke it in the conversation above and superimposed on the spectrogram is the pitch as it varies with time. In contrast, the lower part of Fig. 8.4 shows the same phrase spoken as if there were only two possible choices: ham or chicken and nothing else. The different intonation patterns are very clear.

If synthetic speech is to sound natural in the context of a conversation, the prosody should help to reinforce the communicative intent. Speaking a list of choices is admittedly a rather special case, and I signal this with an explicit focus in the user intent, i.e. *Inform(List)*. Nevertheless, if I always used a very neutral prosody in the form of a gently falling pitch with little deviation, then my voice would be rather boring, and it would make it harder for Steve to follow the conversation.

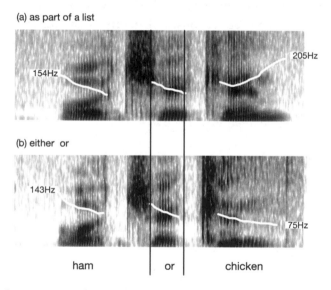

Figure 8.4 *Spectrogram with superimposed pitch contour of the phrase "ham or chicken" spoken (a) as part of a list or (b) as either–or alternatives.*

Controlling the fine details of prosody is very difficult, and prosodic errors are jarring to a human listener. So rather than attempting to manipulate prosody directly, for example by explicitly specifying pitch contours, I condition my synthesiser in a more indirect way using *prosodic styles*.

A prosodic style is a vector which determines one particular mix of prosodic features.[4] These prosodic styles are learned automatically during training and then combined to form a *prosody control vector* which is input to the synthesis decoder alongside the *context vector* (see Fig. 8.3). By adding multiple styles together in differing proportions, I can achieve a wide range of prosodic effects.

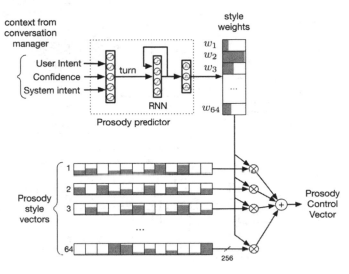

Figure 8.5 *Controlling prosody by selecting style vectors.*

I illustrate the basic scheme in Fig. 8.5. At each turn of the conversation, I input the context signals from my conversation manager to a *prosody predictor* network. This is a recurrent network which tracks the conversation at the intent level. Every turn, the hidden state of the recurrent network is input to a feed-forward network with a softmax output layer to generate a set of weights corresponding to each of my 64 prosodic style vectors. Each prosodic vector is then scaled by the corresponding weight and summed together to form the prosody control vector which conditions my speech synthesis decoder as it generates the mel-spectrogram (see Fig. 8.3).

As I mentioned earlier, I train the prosodic style vectors and the prosody predictor network together with the main speech synthesiser. An overview of the training set-up is shown in Fig. 8.6. The idea is to learn a set of prosody style vectors which can cover all of the prosodic patterns encountered in the training data. To do this a *prosody encoder* is introduced, which is trained to output style vector weights directly from the training mel-spectrograms. The prosody predictor is trained in parallel to mimic the prosody encoder but using the context signals as input rather than the mel-spectrogram.

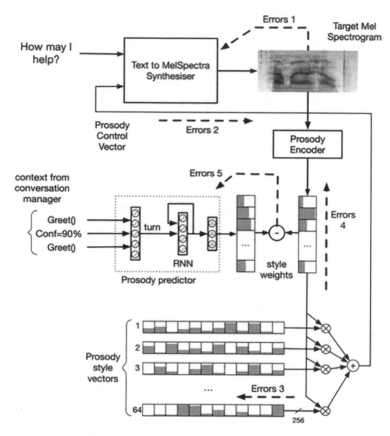

Figure 8.6 *Training the prosody control system.*

The top part of the figure shows the main synthesiser. The training sample is the utterance "How may I help?" and the corresponding target mel-spectrogram is derived directly from the speech of my training speaker. The errors between the predicted mel-spectrogram and the target are back-propagated through the synthesiser network to adjust the weights of the synthesiser encoder–decoder. These are shown as Errors 1 in the diagram.

The target mel-spectrogram is also input to a prosody encoder to predict a set of style vector weights. This encoder consists of a convolutional network to extract features from the spectrogram followed by a recurrent network and a feed-forward network with a softmax output similar to the prosody predictor. The prosody encoder and the style vectors are trained along with the main synthesiser using the errors back-propagated via the prosody control vector connection shown as Errors 2 in the diagram which splits into Errors 3 to adjust the values in the style vectors and Errors 4 to adjust the weights in the prosody encoder.

In parallel but separately to all of the above, the weights predicted by the prosody encoder are used as targets to compute errors to train the prosody predictor network; these are shown as Errors 5 in the diagram. As the prosody encoder is required only for training, once training is complete, it is discarded.

Since the prosody style vectors are trained automatically without explicit labels, it is hard to identify exactly what each one does. However, if I ignore the prosody predictor and sample the style vectors one by one, I find that some vectors speed up my speech and others slow it down. Some styles generate distinct pitch contours and others change the overall voice quality. For example, lack of confidence is signalled by a tension in the voice and higher than average pitch. Setting the prosody control vector to zero results in a uniformly neutral voice.

8.5   Generating the Waveform

In order for Steve to actually hear me, I have to convert my synthesised mel-spectrograms into waveforms that I can send to my audio output channel.[5] Remember that a mel-spectrogram consists of a sequence of vectors where each vector represents a 10-millisecond slice of the spectrogram and a waveform consists of a sequence of numbers representing the amplitude at successive moments in time. So this might seem like yet another sequence-to-sequence problem. However, the sequences in this case are much too long to embed the entire input and then generate the entire output, and in any case, embedding the whole sequence is unnecessary since each spectral vector corresponds to exactly 160 samples. So instead I have trained a convolutional network to generate waveforms sample by sample conditioned on a single spectral vector. I start the decoder generating samples using the first spectral vector of the mel-spectrogram and then replace this vector every 160 samples. When the end of the spectrogram is reached, the decoder stops.

An overview of the generation process is shown in Fig. 8.7. The waveform being generated is shown in the upper part of the figure. The range of possible waveform amplitudes is divided into 1,024 distinct levels. Each waveform sample is assigned to the nearest level and then encoded as a 1-hot vector. Each new sample of the waveform is predicted

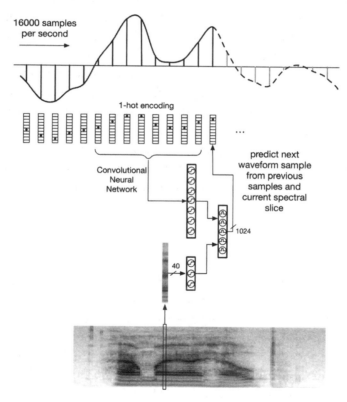

Figure 8.7 *Synthesising waveforms sample by sample.*

based on the current spectral vector processed by a regular feed-forward network and a window of the most recently generated samples processed by a convolutional network.

Just as a language model must be able to generate all plausible sentences of a language, the convolutional network should be able to generate waveforms with all of the characteristics of natural speech. In order to do this, the window of preceding samples input to the convolutional network needs to stretch back over several hundred samples and it also needs to be quite deep.

If a regular network structure was used there would be too many weights to train and it would take too long to compute when I want to talk. So instead I use the so-called *dilated* convolutional structure illustrated in Fig. 8.8. For clarity, this diagram shows just four layers, and just one convolutional neuron at each layer. In fact there are 18 layers and 32 neurons in each layer.[6]

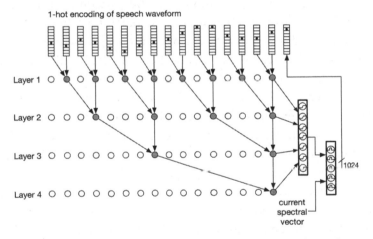

Figure 8.8 *The dilated convolutional network structure used to extend the prediction window back in time.*

Each circle in the figure represents the output of the convolutional neuron at each level and for each waveform sample. There is no pooling as in previous cases of using convolutional neurons. Every neuron has an input window spanning just two input samples. In the first layer, the two input samples are the actual waveform samples and they are adjacent. In layer 2, the two input samples are taken from the features output by layer 1, but instead of taking adjacent features, every second feature is used. In layer 3, every fourth feature is used and in layer 4, every eighth feature is used. This gives an effective window size of 16 but, as can be seen by considering the neurons in grey, the calculation of the neuron outputs at the current time step depends on only a few of the neurons within that window. In the picture, the current step depends on only 11 of the 60 preceding neuron outputs in the window and in deeper networks this ratio is even smaller. Since a typical 5-second utterance requires me to repeat this calculation 80,000 times, using these dilated convolutional neurons is a great help. I still need some computational tricks to be able to speak in real time, but the dilated structure reduces the computational load significantly without affecting accuracy.[7]

The net effect of this dilated convolutional structure is that, using relatively few parameters, the model can take account of a significant amount of history. In my actual waveform generator, I have 18 layers of neurons organised into three cycles of dilations, giving me an effective window of 384 samples. Notice also in Fig. 8.8 that I utilise the outputs of the neurons in the current time slice at every level to predict the next sample. This allows the network to take account of both low- and high-level signal features. The model is trained using the same data as the main synthesiser. Each utterance is input to the network along with its mel-spectrogram and the errors between each predicted sample and the actual sample are back-propagated. In normal use each new predicted sample is appended to the waveform to become an input for the next sample prediction. As in my speech recogniser and response generator, I use a teacher mode in the early stages of training, in which the actual waveform sample is appended to reduce the cumulative effect of prediction errors.

As I have already mentioned, my native language is English and since my language understanding and generation components are intimately linked to my knowledge graph, it would be a substantial amount of work for me to move to another language. However, as you have seen, apart from handling language-specific symbols such as dates and times, there is very little that is language-specific about the way that I recognise and synthesise speech. All I need are audio recordings and the corresponding transcriptions, and I have these for quite a few languages, 29 at the last count! So whilst I think in the English language, I can actually recognise and speak many others. One way in which I can take advantage of this linguistic dexterity is by using my translation skills.

Chapter 9

How Do You Say That In … ?

Being able to recognise and speak a language without understanding anything would not seem to be a terribly useful skill. However, I can also translate between English and any of the other 28 languages. So at minimum I am useful as an interpreter. Let me demonstrate …

Steve, may I remind you it's your godson's birthday tomorrow?
Thanks Cyba, I had forgotten.
Do you want me to send him an eCard?
Yes, tell him "Have a great day." In German, of course.
"And I am looking forward to seeing you next summer."
Ok, so that's "Ich wünsche Ihnen einen wunderbaren Tag."
"Und ich freue mich auf ein Wiedersehen im nächsten Sommer."
If you say so, Cyba, my German is not so great.
No problem, I will send it now.

You won't be surprised to learn that I use an encoder–decoder model to translate from one language to another but, as with all applications of this technology, there are specific issues that need to be addressed. So let me tell you more about how I do this.

You will by now be very familiar with the idea of using an encoder–decoder architecture to translate from one kind of sequence into another. My speech recogniser uses it to convert spectral vectors into words;

my conversation manager uses a variant of it to convert dialogue acts into responses; and my speech synthesiser uses it to convert words into sounds. So it won't be a big surprise to learn that my ability to translate from one language into another also depends on an encoder–decoder architecture.

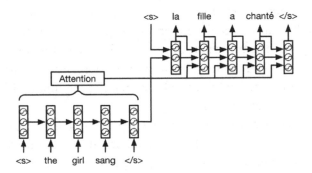

Figure 9.1 *Neural machine translation using an encoder–decoder with attention.*

Indeed, it was machine translation that motivated the development of neural sequence-to-sequence models in the first place.[1] The basic idea is illustrated in Fig. 9.1. The input sentence in the source language is encoded into a sequence of hidden states and the decoder is initialised with the final hidden state and a start-of-sentence marker. The decoder then generates the translation in the target language word by word, conditioned at each step by a context vector formed by attending over the encoder states. The model is trained using a corpus of so-called "parallel texts" comprising texts in the source language and their translations in the target language. The parameters of the model are trained by back-propagating the error between the reference translation and the predicted translation.

This simple model works quite well. However, there are some issues which limit its effectiveness in practice: the need for more efficient and effective encoding, the handling of rare words and the need to provide multi-lingual operation. Also, as with all encoder–decoder systems, generating the most likely translation does not always provide the best result. Let's look at each of these issues in turn.

9.1 Transformer Networks

Recurrent neural networks process sequences by combining the input at each turn with a copy of the previous output. In principle, this recurrence allows a recurrent network to integrate and record information over the entire history of a sequence regardless of its length. In Fig. 9.1 the decoder is initialised with the final hidden state of the encoder and this should be sufficient to enable the entire output sequence to be decoded. However, in practice, information processed early in the input sequence is soon forgotten. Hence the initialisation is augmented by an attention mechanism which attempts to track that part of the input which is most relevant to the current decoder output.

There is a second problem with recurrent networks. Since the processing of each input symbol in a sequence depends on the previous symbol, the computation is inherently sequential. Training data-sets are very large, and growing larger by the day. Back home in the cloud there are hundreds of processing units that I can use and it would be great if I could exploit multiple processing units in parallel in order to train on data more efficiently. However, the sequential constraints of recurrent networks prevent me from doing this.

Given that attention can examine any state of the input, I had been wondering for a while whether hidden state feedback is needed at all. After recently receiving an upgrade in which my recurrent network-based machine translation circuitry was replaced by a new type of sequence to sequence model, I am excited to report that attention is indeed all that you need![2]

These new types of sequence processor are called *transformer networks* and they have no recurrent units. Instead they use something called self-attention in order to encode each symbol in a sequence taking account of all of its neighbours. Transformer networks make parallel computation much easier and they seem to provide better quality translation, probably because self-attention is more powerful than recurrence for encoding and decoding natural language.

Before I dive into the details of how I use transformer networks for language translation, let me first try to explain the underlying principles, focussing first on encoding. Fig. 9.2 shows the sequence of embeddings corresponding to the sentence "The girl sang" with start and end markers

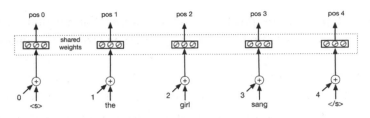

Figure 9.2 *Skeleton of a transformer network.*

being input to a very rudimentary skeletal transformer. Each element has its position marked by adding an embedding which encodes its index in the sequence. This position-augmented embedding is then input to a feed-forward network whose weights are shared across all positions. The outputs at each position then encode the input symbol and its position in the sequence. These outputs are similar to the hidden states of a recurrent network, but a transformer only seeks to extract features from the input sequence and encode them in another sequence of the same length. There is no recurrence and no equivalent to a final state and hence there is no explicit embedding of the input sequence.

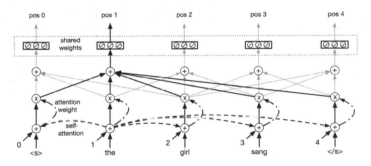

Figure 9.3 *Skeleton of transformer network with self-attention.*

This rudimentary transformer encodes its inputs independently of their neighbours and, as we know, the ability to encode context is crucial for language understanding and indeed most sequence processing tasks. This ability is incorporated into a transformer by allowing each input to self-attend over all of the other inputs. I'll show you in detail how this works shortly, but first look at Fig. 9.3, which is a modified version of Fig. 9.2 in which the input to the output layer is now a weighted sum of all of the inputs. Using position 1 as an example, the position 1 marked input embedding is compared with the position marked embeddings of all of the inputs (including itself). You can think of this as position 1 querying all of the other positions to ask how relevant they are to its own encoding. A query to position k generates an attention weight which is a measure of how relevant position k is to position 1. These weights are then used to compute the weighted sum of inputs for position 1. The same calculation is applied to all input positions to generate the output sequence, which now encodes each position marked input symbol in context, and since the position calculations are independent of each other, they can be computed in parallel.

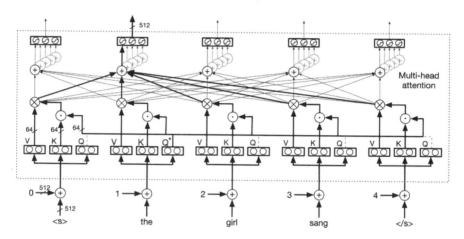

Figure 9.4 *Input layer of encoder shown in Fig. 9.6.*

Let's now take a deeper look at how the self-attention works. Fig. 9.4 shows the same example again, but it now includes all of the required neural circuitry. Each position marked input embedding is input to three linear networks, i.e. networks without a squashing function, labelled V, K and Q in the diagram, which stand for value, key and query. Value is the contribution of the input at that position that will be weighted and passed through to the output. The key is a vector used to determine the relevance of this position in response to a query vector from this or any other position in the sequence. To compute the output for position 1, the query output Q^* is compared with the key values of all positions, including its own. Each comparison is computed using a dot-product, and the result is an attention weight which is then used to scale the corresponding value.

This figure also shows the dimensions of the transformer network that I actually use in my language translator. As you can see, the input embeddings are of dimension 512, whereas the value vector is only of dimension 64. The reason for this reduction is that there are in fact eight self-attention networks in parallel. Each network has different parameters and learns to represent different relations in the data. All 8 of these attention-weighted values are input to the output layer, making 512 inputs in total. This so-called *multi-headed* attention is the main source of the transformer network's representational power.

In the description above, I skipped over the issue of how to embed the input position. This embedding could be generated by a feed-forward network which takes as input the binary input position and outputs a vector of size equal to the input symbol embeddings. It would then be trained by error back propagation along with all of the other network weights. The problem with this is that my training data consists of relatively short sequences and a learned position embedding might fail if at run-time I was asked to translate a long passage of text. So instead I use the sinusoidal pattern shown in Fig. 9.5, where each vertical stripe is a position embedding. The leftmost stripe corresponds to position 0, the next stripe corresponds to position 1, and so on. Each horizontal row corresponds to successive elements of the embedding.

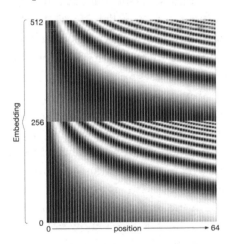

Figure 9.5 *Sinusoidal registration pattern encoding symbol position in a sequence.*

In the upper half the rows are sine waves and in the lower half the rows are cosine waves. In both cases, the frequency of the wave increases with each successive row.

I expect you are wondering what is special about this pattern. Well, firstly it can be extended indefinitely and each successive vertical slice will continue to be unique. Secondly, it can be shown that for any position k, the encoded position of a near neighbour at $k + \delta$ can be expressed as a simple linear function of the encoding at k. This allows the attention mechanism to learn relationships with nearby symbols as a function of their relative distance δ rather than their absolute positions.

9.2 Using a Transformer Network for Language Translation

The architecture of my new neural language translation system using transformer networks is shown in Fig. 9.6. The input sequence is encoded using multiple identical layers (in this case six). Each layer consists of a sub-layer of self-attention followed by a feed-forward network exactly as I described in the previous section.

The decoder is identical to the encoder except that each layer has a second attention sub-layer sitting on top of the self-attention sub-layer. This second layer operates like a conventional attention mechanism, attending over the outputs of the encoder. In operation, all encoder positions can be computed in parallel. However, the decoder must still generate the translated output sequence symbol by symbol. As with a recurrent network encoder–decoder, the decoder input is initialised with the start-of-sentence symbol "<s>". Position 0 of the decoder can then be calculated, generating the output "la". However, since the rest of the sequence is unknown at this point, position 0 can only self-attend to itself. The generated output "la" is added to the input and the process is repeated. This time position 1 can self-attend to itself and all previously generated positions, which is just position 0 in this case. This repeats until the end-of-sentence symbol "</s>" is generated.

When training, both the encoder positions and the decoder positions can be computed in parallel because I know both the input sequence and the target output sequence. So I process all input symbols in parallel, starting with the input layer and working up to the final output. Once the

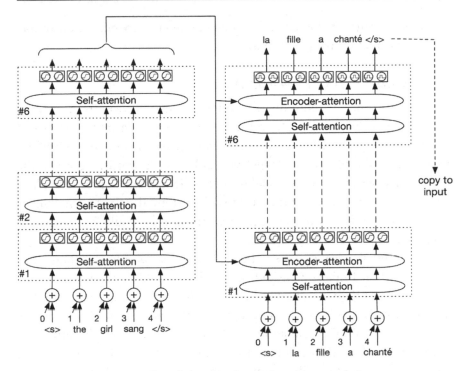

Figure 9.6 *Transformer-based neural machine translation.*

encoding is complete, the decoder can be processed in exactly the same way, provided that the self-attention layers are prevented from examining output symbols that have not been generated yet. This can be done by simply masking-out all future decoder input positions.

In summary, a transformer network encodes a sequence by projecting each input embedding into a set of value vectors, a set of query vectors and a set of key vectors using a bank of linear networks. Each bank is referred to as an *attention head*. For each input position, the query vectors are used to scan the entire sequence by matching them with the key vectors of all the other positions. The match scores are then used as attention weights to combine all the value vectors. The summed value vectors for each bank of each position are then input to a feed-forward network to produce the state output for that position. This encoding is repeated for multiple layers to generate the final encoder output. The decoder works in exactly the same way except that it has an encoder attention layer between each self-attention layer and the output network. This system of multi-headed attention is very powerful and it removes the need for a recurrent state, thereby allowing much more efficient training, and better operational performance.

9.3 Characters or Words or ...

Encoder–decoder models operate on sequences drawn from a finite vocabulary of symbols and, for machine translation, the obvious choice of symbol might seem to be the word. Indeed, the examples above implicitly assume that the source and target vocabularies are words. However, the complexity of a translation model is directly dependent on the vocabulary size and in practice computational constraints limit the size to a maximum of 100,000 words. As a consequence, rare words would be treated as unknown and could not be translated.

If my English vocabulary was limited to 100,000 words, less than 1% of the words that I might be asked to translate would be unknown to me, which is potentially acceptable. However, for other languages a limit of 100,000 words would result in a significantly higher out of vocabulary rate. For example, German compound nouns such as Dampfschifffahrts-gesellschaft (steamship company) would be treated as single words and very few of them would be in my vocabulary. Compounds such as these could in principle be handled by pre-processing the input text to identify and split them into their constituent words and then post-processing output texts to rejoin them back together. However, this would require identifying compound nouns and dealing with language-specific features such as knowing when to insert the German *linking-s*.[3] Morphologically rich languages such as Czech, Turkish and Arabic would also require very large vocabularies since words in these languages can have a large number of inflected forms.

Language complexity is not the only problem in using word-based vocabularies. If I had a fixed vocabulary, named entities such as persons and places would usually be out of vocabulary, yet often they could have been just copied over from the source to the target. For example, Barack Obama is the same in most European languages. Copying can also be useful in languages with non-Latin character sets if the translit-eration rules are simple enough for the encoder–decoder to learn. For example, the transliteration of Barack Obama to Russian Барак Обама is relatively simple. Rare words with a common origin can also be handled by copying and transliterating. For example, claustrophobia becomes

Klaustrophobie in German and Клаустрофобия (Klaustrofobiya) in Russian. Even setting aside the complication that many languages such as Chinese and Japanese lack explicit word boundaries, it's clear that choosing words as the fundamental unit of translation is not ideal.

A more flexible choice of fundamental unit would be the character, and indeed character-level coding does deal adequately with the problems outlined above. However, translating from one language to another at the character level requires the model to learn the morphology of the language in addition to the syntax and semantics. This additional learning burden results in a drop in performance compared with word-level translation. Also, coding a source text as a sequence of characters results in very long symbol sequences and this significantly increases the required computation both during training and in operation.

What I really need is some form of intermediate sub-word representation which is easy to compute and language-independent. Various schemes have been proposed for this, with varying degrees of complexity. The one that I use is very simple but nevertheless effective. It is based on a method of compressing messages called *byte pair encoding (BPE)*.[4]

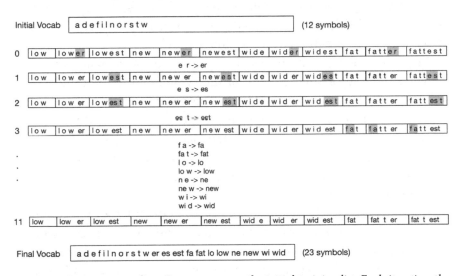

Figure 9.7 *Byte pair encoding. Row 0 represents the initial training list. Each iteration, the most frequent symbol pair is merged to form a new symbol which is added to the vocabulary.*

I illustrate the BPE algorithm in Fig. 9.7, where I assume for the moment that we are encoding a single language. The starting point is to create a list of all of the words in the training data along with their frequency counts and a vocabulary initialised with all the characters used in the training data. In the figure, the training list consists of just 12 words (see row 0) and for the purposes of the illustration there are no repetitions. Coding then proceeds iteratively. At each cycle, the most frequent pair of symbols are merged to form a new symbol which is added to the vocabulary. In cycle 1 of the example, the symbols 'e' and 'r' are the most frequent pair in the training list so they are merged to form a new symbol 'er'. In cycle 2, the symbols 'e' and 's' are merged to form a new symbol 'es' and in cycle 3, the symbols 'es' and 't' are merged to form a new symbol 'est'. This continues until the vocabulary has reached the required size. In the example, the algorithm terminates when 11 new symbols have been added to the vocabulary.

Once the vocabulary has been built, the symbols are stored in descending order of length. A new word is encoded by searching through the vocabulary. If any symbol is a substring of any so far unmatched portion of the word, then that substring is replaced by the symbol. For example, using the vocabulary shown in Fig. 9.7, the word "lowness" would first have "low" replaced by a symbol, then "ne" would be replaced by a symbol and finally each "s" would be replaced by a single character symbol yielding the BPE encoding "low-ne-s-s".

In my actual translation systems, I grow the vocabulary to 32,000 symbols. Not surprisingly, many of the symbols in the vocabulary are common words and common endings. This vocabulary is large enough to cover much of the morphology of the language but, since it includes all of the characters as symbols, it is guaranteed to be capable of encoding any new word requiring translation. Since the encoding process can be quite slow, I save some time by precomputing the encoding for the most commonly used words.

It would be perfectly feasible to train a separate BPE for each language, but lack of consistency might then make it difficult for each encoder–decoder to copy named entities. For example, if "Barack" in English is coded as "Bar-ack" it would be unfortunate if it was coded as "Ba-rack" in German.

To avoid this, I train a single BPE to cover both the source language and the target language by simply merging all of the training data. The initial training list then contains the frequency counts of all words in both languages and the initial vocabulary contains the characters used in both languages. Unlike European languages, Asian languages often have quite large character sets. For example, Japanese consists of a mixture of Kanji, Hiragana and Katakana giving over 20,000 characters in total. For languages like these, I let my BPE-derived vocabulary expand up to 64,000 symbols. Otherwise it would be saturated by individual characters with little opportunity to accrete longer segments.

9.4   Multi-lingual Translation

An obvious approach to supporting multi-lingual translation is to train a separate encoder–decoder for every required language pair. In the general case, supporting N languages would require N^2 models and this is not practical for more than three or four languages. Even if all translations are to or from English as they are in my case, it would require $2N$ models and since I speak 28 languages other than English, even this is impractical.

Instead, I allocate each language to one of 10 groups and train a single encoder–decoder for each group.[5] For example, I have a Germanic group containing Danish, Dutch, Norwegian, Swedish and German; a Romance group containing French, Italian, Portuguese and Spanish; and an Indo-Iranian group containing Hindi, Bengali, Telugu, Farsi and Greek. Yes, Greek does look a bit odd in this group but surprisingly it seems to work well there. English is a member of every group and all training data contains English as one of the translation pairs.

To train each group, all of the training data is merged into a single pool and a single BPE is constructed to cover the whole group. The encoder–decoder is then trained by repeatedly selecting a random batch of training pairs from the pool and updating the model. In each training pair, a symbol identifying the target language is prepended to the source language. Once the model is trained, I can translate English into any other language in the group by prepending the appropriate language identifier to the start of the English text.

Generally speaking, the multi-lingual models trained in this rather simplistic manner have similar performance to individual encoder-decoders trained on a single language pair. A single multi-lingual encoder–decoder has to absorb much more information about the mappings between languages but it benefits from seeing more data regarding common features across the group. It also sees much more English data, so translations into English benefit from a stronger language model. Overall, these things seem to balance out. An interesting side effect is that if a translation group contains the language pairs English $\leftrightarrow$ X and English $\leftrightarrow$ Y, then I can make a passable job of translating directly between X and Y even though I have no training data pairs for X $\leftrightarrow$ Y.

9.5 Beam Search

As with all encoder–decoder architectures, my transformer-based decoder generates the output sequence symbol by symbol. Primed with a start symbol, it predicts the probability of each possible next symbol based on the previously generated sequence. Selecting the most likely symbol at each step generates the most likely symbol sequence. However, as with my speech recogniser, performance can be improved by generating a *beam* of the most likely candidate translations and then rescoring them to account for additional information. For each candidate, I first normalise the likelihood score to produce an average likelihood per symbol. This avoids penalising long sequences. Secondly, I want to make sure that my translation takes account of all of the symbols in the source text, so I add a *coverage score* to the average likelihood and use this new combined score to find the best candidate.

The coverage score plays a similar role to the output token tracker that I use in my response generator. However, here I don't have an encoding of the underlying meaning. Instead, I use a softer measure based on the attention weights. Each symbol of the target translation attends over the symbols of the source, and for any target symbol the sum of the weights is 1 by design. However, the sum of the weights referring to any given source symbol can range from 0 to the number of symbols in the target. For good coverage, I would like to be reassured that the decoder paid some attention to all source symbols.

A simple way of measuring this is to compute the sum of the attention weights for each source symbol but limit the sum to 1. Then the source symbol attention normalised by the length of the target can be used as a

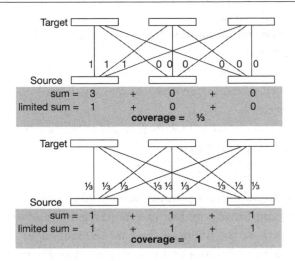

Figure 9.8 *Measuring coverage from attention weights.*

coverage score. This is illustrated in Fig. 9.8, which shows in stylised form three source symbols translated to three target symbols with the attention weights between them. The example at the top of the figure shows an extreme case where all of the attention is on the first source symbol. The sum of the weights on this symbol is 3 but this is reduced to 1 by the symbol limit. The total sum is therefore 1, which, when normalised by the number of symbols in the target, gives a coverage score of $\frac{1}{3}$. In contrast, the example at the bottom of the figure shows the other extreme where the attention is evenly spread over all symbols. In this case, the sum at each symbol is 1 and the limit does not apply. The resulting coverage score in this case is 1. In practice, the coverage score will vary between the two extreme cases depicted in Fig. 9.8. When combined with the normalised likelihood in the proportions 80% and 20%, I find that rescoring makes a small but appreciable improvement to the overall quality of my translations.

9.6 The Limits of Neural Machine Translation

Before leaving the topic of machine translation, it is worth reflecting on the limits of the neural network technology that I use. Just a minute ...

Steve, you have a new message from your godson.
Ok, read it to me.
Danke für die E-Karte. Ich freue mich auf den Sommer,
wenn wir wieder Tennis spielen können.
In English please!
Thanks for the e-card. I'm looking forward to the summer
when we can play tennis again.

Generally, the translations I produce of everyday simple sentences like this message from Steve's godson are pretty good, and usually understandable by a listener fluent in the target language. However, the encoder–decoder architecture that I employ is trained to map one surface form into another without attempting to understand anything about the underlying communicative intent. The weaknesses of this strategy are easily exposed.

Let's take a simple example. If I translate into German[6]

In their house, everything comes in pairs. There's his car and her car, his towels and her towels, and his library and hers.

I produce

In ihrem Haus kommt alles paarweise. Da sind sein Auto und ihr Auto, seine Handtücher und ihre Handtücher, und seine Bibliothek und ihre.

This translation is acceptable because the possessives "his" and "her" have direct equivalents in German and the intended contrast between his and her carries over. Translating into French is not so easy, however, because the form of possessive in French depends on the object of the possession not the subject as in English and German. So for French I generate

Dans leur maison, tout vient par paires. Il y a sa voiture et sa voiture, ses serviettes et ses serviettes, et sa bibliothèque et la sienne.

which makes little sense because I have no ability to understand that the second sentence is meant to be providing examples of the first statement that everything in their house comes in pairs.

This is just one of the many constructions that are routinely used in literary works. They are effective because you humans understand not just the words but the underlying ideas. I cannot do that, so be warned that asking me to translate literary prose is unlikely to produce a good outcome!

Chapter *10*

Let's Chat

One moment . . .

Hey Cyba, read me John Agoulis's bio on Wikipedia.
Ok Steve. John Agoulis, born in 1964, is CEO of SmartCo.
He cofounded SmartCo in 2012 and has been its CEO since inception.
He studied Electrical Engineering at MIT and an MBA at Wharton.
His hobby is winemaking and he owns a small vineyard in
Sonoma County.
What grape varieties are planted in Sonoma County?
According to the web, the most common varieties are Chardonnay,
Cabernet Sauvignon and Pinot noir.
Which is the most expensive?
Some of the most coveted and expensive bottles of Sonoma County
wine are Chardonnay.
Ok, thanks.

Hmm, Steve seems to be prepping himself with some background ready for his 9pm telephone call. I don't have anything in my knowledge graph about grapes or Sonoma County so this last exchange is an example of me talking about something that I don't know anything about. Steve seemed to think my response was reasonable but nevertheless this kind of exchange is outside of my core competence. For me it is chit-chat and a prime example of me appearing to be smarter than I really am. Nevertheless, chit-chat can serve a useful purpose, so let me tell you more about it.

I refer to all interactions which lie outside of the domain of my conversation manager as *chit-chat*. Although chit-chat is not part of my core remit, it still has a purpose. Often chit-chat provides useful information, albeit unverified, as in the example above, and other times it provides some harmless amusement for Steve. Chit-chat also plays a role in adding colour to my personality, which is important both for making me an effective personal assistant and for helping to engender trust.

I explained in Chapter 7 the role of my conversation manager in orchestrating the interactions between Steve and myself. These interactions involve building explicit interpretations of input utterances called intent graphs, executing these graphs against my knowledge graph, constructing responses in the form of dialogue acts and then rendering these responses via text into speech. At the core of this processing is my knowledge graph. I endeavour to keep my knowledge graph as accurate as possible so that when I convey information, I have some confidence in its accuracy. However, although it is quite large, my knowledge graph is not infinite.

When Steve asked me "What grape varieties are planted in Sonoma County?," I identified "Sonoma County" as a named entity but I couldn't find it in my knowledge graph. However, when I used the sentence as a web search query, I found lots of documents relating to this question, so I scanned them, extracted individual sentences and then chose the one which seemed most likely to be a good response to the question. My actual response was probably helpful; however, I had no idea what I said to him nor could I place any confidence in its accuracy. I tried to signal this by prepending "According to the web ...". Furthermore, since I had no explicit representation of the entities and relations involved, I couldn't provide accurate follow-up information when Steve asked "Which is the most expensive?" All I could do instead was resubmit an expanded web search query with the previous response and the follow-up query appended. The result "Some of the most coveted and expensive bottles of Sonoma County wine are Chardonnay." was vaguely relevant but didn't really answer the question. Indeed, it was somewhat misleading since Cabernet Sauvignon is actually the most expensive grape in Sonoma.

Just a minute, Steve now seems to be killing time until his 9pm telephone call ...

Hey Cyba, what does Cyba mean.
Hi Steve, it means like it sounds. [hc]
Really! Do you have a hobby Cyba?
I like to listen to jazz music. [ed]
<pause>
Do you have a hobby Steve? [hc]
I like to cook.
What's your favourite cuisine? [rb]
Italian, both to eat and to cook.
Do you go to cooking classes? [rb]
Yes, in London.
Hmm, pricey I bet but worth it. [rb]
Yes, they are excellent.
That's good to know. [ed]

Generating responses from web-search is just one of the techniques I use to support chit-chat. I have four in total and this last exchange illustrates the other three, which I have labelled in square brackets.

My first response was generated by a *hand-crafted* generator [hc] which can handle a variety of the stock questions which humans seem unable to resist asking me such as what does my name mean, and where was I born. It can also provide continuity by helping to keep the conversation moving when Steve doesn't respond as expected, as in the third turn above. My second response was generated by an *encoder–decoder* [ed] trained on human–human conversation augmented by some personal information to colour my personality. Turns four, five and six were generated by a *retrieval-based* generator [rb] which uses the current dialogue context to search a database of stored responses. I'll explain first how these work together and then describe each one in more detail.

10.1   My Chatty Responders

The four response generators that I use for chit-chat are shown in Fig. 10.1. Each turn the current input plus the sequence of words spanning the dialogue history is input to each generator. A selector module decides which response is most appropriate and passes the selected response to a filter that ensures that the response does not contain offensive material and also applies some simple rule-based edits such as prepending phrases like "According to the web" and "Did you know that" in order to improve the coherence of the conversation.

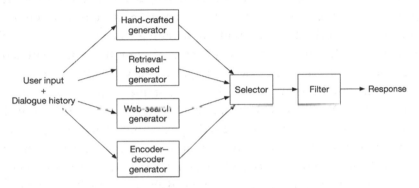

Figure 10.1 *Response modules supporting chit-chat.*

The hand-crafted response generator has limited scope and it is unable to maintain a multi-turn conversation. As soon as Steve responds to a question from me or volunteers a topic of his own accord then I need to provide him with more substantive responses, and this requires access to data. Fortunately, the huge popularity of social media sites and public forums such as Facebook, Twitter, Reddit, etc. means that millions of humans are chatting to each other via text messages every day. Some of this data, suitably anonymised and filtered, can be used by conversational agents such as myself to improve their chatting skills.[1]

There are two different ways in which I use conversational data. Firstly, I use it to create a database of stored responses. When I get a question or comment, I search this database for the closest matching response and output it verbatim. This provides the basis of my retrieval-based generator. Secondly, I use the data to train an encoder–decoder to generate responses directly from inputs in just the same way that my machine translation encoder–decoder transforms one language into another. My web-search generator follows a similar pattern to the retrieval-based generator except that its data source is the web itself.

10.2 Hand-Crafted Response Generation

My hand-crafted response generator was inspired by a program called Eliza which was written by an MIT computer scientist called Joe Weizen-baum in the mid 1960s.[2] Eliza was designed to simulate a psychother-apist and, although very simple, it can nevertheless appear to be quite intelligent. It works by using pattern matching rules to extract specific phrases from the input utterance and then copying them into templated responses.[3] In Eliza, these rules were particularly effective at reflecting back whatever the user says to it. For example, if the user says "I'm worried about X," Eliza might respond "Why are you worried about X?" I use a similar technique for deflecting questions that I don't wish to answer whilst keeping the conversation moving. For example, I have a rule for "Who is your favourite X?" which generates the response "I don't have a favourite X. Who is yours?" In the exchange with Steve above, the pattern "Do you have a X, Cyba?" triggered the response "Do you have a X, Steve?"

In addition to these continuity rules which are designed to keep the conversation alive, I also have a large number of rules which generate *canned responses*. They were provided by my human designers to serve a number of purposes. Firstly, they handle questions in areas such as race, sex and religion, whose responses need to be chosen very carefully. Usu-ally these are as neutral and unprovocative as possible, though sometimes I head off the question with an attempt at humour. Steve has never said "Hey Cyba, talk dirty to me." but if he did my response would be "Ok, humus, compost, pumice, silt, gravel." (this was borrowed from my cousin Siri). Secondly, they allow me to respond appropriately to joke questions such as "Will you go out with me?," "Have you ever been in love?" and "Can time go backwards?" The response to Steve asking me what my name means was an example of this. Finally, a few of my canned responses are designed to flatter Steve, since it has been shown that humans enjoy flattery from computers as much as from other humans![4]

10.3   Retrieval-Based Response Generation

Most of my responses are not "canned," because the number of possible questions I could be asked is infinite. Most of the time when I am chatting I use retrieval-based responses, either from an internal database like the one I collected from conversations on social media sites or by searching the web. I illustrate the basic idea of retrieval-based response generation in Fig. 10.2. Each response line in a database of responses has an associated sentence-level embedding. To generate a response at runtime, the last user input and the dialogue history are encoded to yield a complimentary embedding which is then matched via a dot-product with the embeddings of each candidate response in the database. I then select the response with the largest dot-product as the best response.

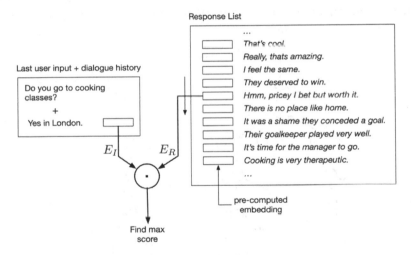

Figure 10.2 *Retrieval-based response generation.*

There are many possible approaches to computing a sentence-level embedding. I used to use a recurrent network but, as with my machine translation circuitry, my retrieval encoder was recently upgraded to a transformer network using the dual sentence encoder configuration shown in Fig. 10.3.[5] The actual transformer set-up is identical to the encoder side of my neural machine translation encoder–decoder, which I showed in Fig. 9.4, including the use of byte pair encoding for the input text.

In order to form a sentence-level embedding, the encoder outputs corresponding to each input position are summed and then scaled to normalise for utterance length. The dialogue history consists of the utterances from both me and Steve preceding Steve's last input truncated to a maximum of 32 BPE symbols. So for example, when Steve told me that he liked "Italian, both to eat and cook", the truncated dialogue history was "like to listen to jazz music. Do you have a hobby Steve? I like to cook? What's your favourite cuisine?"

The history is encoded separately from the last user input and the output embeddings are averaged to form the final embedding. The transformer parameters are shared across the three input encoders in order to focus on extracting the relevant linguistic features. Each of the output feed-forward networks has its own parameters, and their job is to learn the relationship between the input, dialogue history and response in chit-chat style conversations.

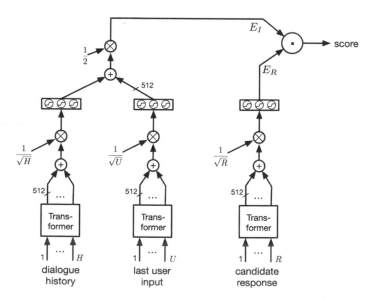

Figure 10.3 *Dual sentence encoder.*

The dual sentence encoder is trained using a corpus of dialogues extracted from social media sites, primarily Reddit. Each turn of a Reddit or other social media dialogue provides a training sample consisting of the dialogue history up to that turn, the current utterance as input and the next utterance as the response. The encoder is trained to identify the actual response from a pool of 50 incorrect responses selected at random from the training set.

You might think that a simpler alternative would be to train the dual sentence encoder to match similar inputs rather than match an input with a response. However, this would not work well in practice because many responses can apply equally well to a diverse range of inputs which have little similarity to each other. For example, it would be hard to find any similarity between "George Best scored a double hat-trick" and "Sunsets on Mars are blue" but the response "That's amazing!" is equally valid for both.

The ability to precompute the response embeddings means that to find the best response I only have to compute the embedding for the input and then search for the response with the largest dot-product. Although I have around a million possible responses to search through, there are various computational tricks that I can use to do the search very quickly and in practice, there is no discernible delay.[6]

10.4 *Web-Search Response Generation*

I generate responses from web queries using the same dual sentence encoder as for retrieval-based response generation. I illustrate the process in Fig. 10.4. The most recent user input is treated as a web query and sent to a standard search engine. If there was a previous query in the conversation, the response to that query is appended to the current query in order to support follow-up questions. For example, in the earlier conversation with Steve about grapes, the query "Which is the most expensive?" was input to the search engine as "The most common varieties are Chardonnay, Cabernet Sauvignon and Pinot noir. Which is the most expensive?"

The top-ranked pages retrieved from the web search are then processed to extract well-formed sentences. These sentences are filtered by my speech recognition language model to create a pool of potential responses. This pool is then scanned by the dual encoder to find the best scoring response. Unlike the retrieval-based response generator, the embeddings of the candidate responses cannot be precomputed. However, the list of candidates is very much shorter, so this is not a problem.

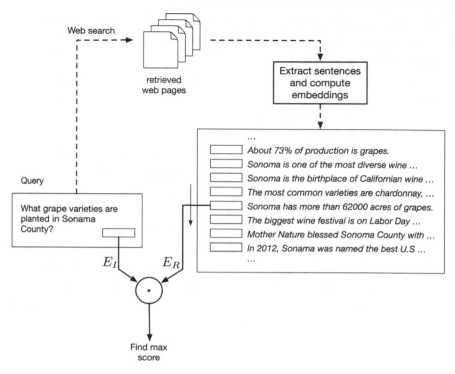

Figure 10.4 *Web search response generation.*

The dual sentence encoder is trained on very large quantities of human–human chit-chat. This allows the transformer networks to learn a good deal about conversational language, but it is not an ideal basis for selecting good responses to web queries since the text in web pages is very different from social media chit-chat. To deal with this, I use a process of *fine tuning* to improve the quality of my web-based responses. Over a period of time I recorded the results of my web searches and, for each query, human annotators marked the sentence which they judged to be the best response. I then used this as training data to update the output feed-forward networks of the dual encoder, leaving the transformer networks unchanged.

10.5 Encoder–Decoder Response Generation

To answer questions such as "Do you have a hobby" I use the encoder–decoder response generator shown in Fig. 10.5, where it is in the process

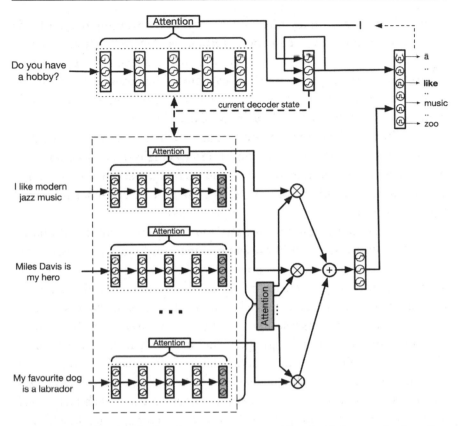

Figure 10.5 *Encoder–decoder-based response generator with embedded personal information.*

of generating a response to this question. The core of this generator is a conventional encoder–decoder with attention as shown at the top of the figure. It is exactly the same as used in many machine translation applications (see Fig. 9.1). It uses simple word-based input and output encoding and it is trained on a subset of the chit-chat corpus used to train my dual sentence encoder plus several data sets derived from spoken conversations. Responses are generated word by word, conditioned on the previous output and a context vector formed by attending over the input. Multiple outputs are generated using a beam search, and the most likely candidate is selected after normalising for sentence length to avoid a bias towards short utterances.

When used in conversation, responses from an encoder–decoder generator are usually acceptable but, because the decoder has to integrate over the very large range of responses seen in the training data, it tends to focus on frequently seen generic responses. A conversation based on this kind of generator alone would be dull and inconsequential. However, my retrieval-based generators are capable of bringing interest to the conversation, so when they are all combined they provide a reasonable balance between fluency and meaningful content.

Something still lacking, however, is any indication of my personality. Of course, I am just a machine and I don't actually have a personality. Nevertheless, humans like to discuss and exchange personal interests and whilst I don't actually have any, for the purpose of chit-chat it helps if I pretend that I do!

There is some personal information in the rules of my hand-crafted generator, but these result in the same canned responses every time they are triggered. I must also be able to weave this personal information seamlessly into a conversation. To do this, I augment the standard encoder–decoder structure with a hierarchical copying mechanism which allows a variety of facts relating to my personal interests to be encoded as statements in natural language.[7] This is shown in the lower half of Fig. 10.5. Each fact such as "I like modern jazz music" is encoded by a recurrent network. When a response is being generated, the current decoder state is used to attend over the hidden states of each fact as well as the current input. This generates a context vector per fact. In addition, the decoder state also attends over the final states of each fact (shown in grey) to provide higher-level attention weights over the facts themselves. The fact context vectors are then summed, weighted by these higher-level fact weights to form a second state vector which is combined with the decoder hidden state as a second input to the output softmax network, providing a probability distribution over the output vocabulary.

The net effect of this neural machinery is that whenever the decoder generates a response related to one or more of the stored facts, its hidden state is augmented by a context vector relating to that fact. This results in keywords and phrases from the stored facts being interspersed in the output. In the earlier exchange with Steve, the question "Do you have a hobby?" triggered the response "I like to listen to music." Presumably, when the topic of hobbies occurs in the training data, listening to music is a common response. The decoder hidden state has learned to include the possibility of outputting the phrase "listen to music" along with many other possible responses. However, this triggers a strong attention signal from the relevant fact overriding the other possibilities and causing the response "I like to listen to jazz music." These personal facts are fixed and I do not record mentions of them to Steve. So if he chatted to me all the time, he might start to find me somewhat repetitive. In practice, it seems that they pop-up sufficiently rarely that this is not a problem. At least, he hasn't yet said "You told me that already."

10.6   Selecting the Best Response

The final component of my machinery for supporting chit-chat is the response selector which has to select which generator output to choose for the current turn of the dialogue (see again Fig. 10.1). Some conversational agents have trained classifiers for this function, often trained using reinforcement learning with the goal of optimising the user experience.[8] However, I take a simpler approach.[9] If the hand-crafted generator produces an output then it is selected. Otherwise, I use the encoder–decoder generator as a language model to compute the average likelihood of each word in the web-search and the retrieval-based generator responses. If the likelihood of the web-search response exceeds a preset threshold, then it is selected; if the likelihood of the retrieval response exceeds a preset threshold, then it is selected. Otherwise, the encoder–decoder generator output is selected. The rationale is that the hand-crafted generator only triggers under certain well-specified situations, so it should have priority. Otherwise, the retrieval responses are preferred because they tend to be the most informative, provided that they are conversationally and linguistically plausible. The encoder–decoder generator tends to produce less informative responses, but they are always plausible and provide a good background response when nothing else seems to fit.

10.7   Social Chatbots

Chit-chat is not one of my core functions, and although the web-search function is often useful, my support for this kind of interaction is primarily designed to provide some light entertainment and fill-out my personality a little. This is not the case with all conversational agents. Some social chatbots are designed to not only engage and entertain, but also educate and provide useful information. For example, my cousin

Xiaolce is designed to engage and bond with its users in order to establish itself as a reliable and trusted source of information and advice.[10] In operation, Xiaolce maintains an *empathy quotient* constructed from a set of classifiers designed to detect the user's emotion (happy, sad, etc.), the user's reaction (whether positive or negative) and interest in the topic as measured against the user's profile and history. Candidate response scoring of the sort I described in the previous section is then augmented by this empathy quotient with the aim of better engaging with the user. Xiaolce builds on its ability to provide coherent empathetic conversation with a large number of skills which focus on topics ranging from counselling and companionship to instruction on how to perform various tasks.

One moment, I need to remind Steve about his 9pm call ...

Steve, your call with John Agoulis is in fifteen minutes.
Ok, thanks.

One day I may get similar functionality to Xiaolce, but social chatbots are built according to very different design criteria. My aim is to complete the goals that Steve sets for me as quickly and as efficiently as possible. The reward function of my conversation manager is penalised for each turn of the dialogue and rewarded for completing each task. In contrast, social chatbots are usually optimised to prolong conversations as long as possible in order to strengthen their engagement and bond with the user.

Chapter 11

Can You Trust Me?

As a personal assistant, I provide a convenient and easily accessible interface to a wide range of systems and services. Steve doesn't like to type much so he uses me quite a lot and, as my capabilities improve, it is likely that I will become an ever more indispensable part of his life. So what are the risks involved and is his trust in me well-placed?

Whether deliberately or inadvertently, there is certainly potential for me to do harm. I have access to a number of on-line accounts, including his bank account, with the power to buy goods and make payments, so there is ample opportunity for fraud. I have stored in my knowledge graph not only a large number of facts about the world, but also a great deal of private information relating to Steve's daily life. Leaking this information to a third party could be damaging. I search the web and select the information that I present to him with the opportunity to bias his thinking and the decisions that he makes. Finally, I engage in social conversation with him, creating the possibility over time of influencing his opinions on a variety of subjects.

Trust is a difficult and multi-faceted question to which there is no simple answer. Much depends on the integrity of my designers and the teams of developers who update my code and supply me with data; and much depends on one's personal appetite for risk. Nevertheless, the key to making sensible decisions about trust is a good understanding of the risks, how to quantify them and how to mitigate them. Understanding these things allows the right questions to be asked and informed judgements to be made. In this chapter, I will explain these risks in more detail and some of the methods I use to mitigate them.

11.1   Security

Whilst speech is a very convenient medium for communication, it is also very insecure in the sense that anybody can eavesdrop on a conversation and understand it. In order to respond instantly to a request, I have to be listening all of the time and this inevitably means that I can hear everything around me, including private conversations which have nothing to do with me. As you already know, I occasionally record utterances that I have misrecognised in order to update the neural networks in my recogniser. I therefore need to be very careful to avoid inadvertently capturing sensitive information through one of my microphones and then adding it to my training data where it might be listened to by a human annotator or, worse, copied to a third party.

As I explained in Chapter 5, when I am not actively engaged in a conversation, all of my neural circuitry is in *sleep mode* apart from a single detector which has been trained to recognise the phrase "Hey Cyba". Until this wake-up phrase has been detected, all incoming audio is simply ignored. Once awake, I continue to listen until the end of the conversation so that Steve does not have to repeat the wake-up phrase at the start of every utterance. This wake-up detector runs on the local device capturing the audio. The audio is not recorded and it does not go to the cloud. So, provided that the detector only triggers when it is supposed to and that I promptly recognise the end of each conversation, inadvertent eavesdropping is unlikely.

There is a second security risk. If Steve speaks to me through his phone, watch or computer then he will have already authenticated himself by using a password or biometric identifier. However, I also use voice channels which lack built-in authentication. For example, Steve often speaks to me via a smart speaker in his office, which is frequently unattended. This creates an obvious security risk since a third party could interrogate me to access private information or ...

Hey Cyba, send a message to the Board cc Krissa Maru.
Ok Steve. What's the message?
SmartCo offer is $18.50 per share.

> *To Board Members, cc Krissa Maru.*
> *"SmartCo offer is $18.50 per share", Ok?*
> Yes, send it, I'm going home.

---

ask me to read confidential messages such as the one that Steve has just sent!

As you know, I try to guard against imposters, by sending my wake-up phrase to a speaker verification component to check that the voice belongs to Steve. Then and only then do I open the audio channel and send the full utterance to my speech recogniser for processing.

If my wake-up and end-of-conversation detection, and my speaker verification work perfectly, then the risks of eavesdropping or an imposter attack are minimal but, of course, nothing is perfect. False triggers will typically occur once or twice a day and most of them are harmless.[1] End-of-conversation failures occur with similar frequency. Again these are mostly harmless, though they sometimes occur when Steve talks to me and then immediately turns and talks to someone else in his office. However, if I believe Steve is still talking to me, I will try to recognise the speech and act on it. For both false triggers and end-of-conversation failures, I normally respond with an apology for failing to understand the request and this alerts Steve and gives him the opportunity to explicitly tell me to ignore the last input and delete it, as happened this afternoon when Steve was talking to Geena in his office.

The net effect of these measures is that although it is possible for me to input a confidential utterance and log it to a server in the cloud marked for transcription and training, the probability is very small. Furthermore, even if an annotator does listen to confidential material, Steve will be protected by the privacy measures described below. Nevertheless, the only absolutely sure way to prevent any possibility of inadvertent eavesdropping leading to a leakage of confidential information is to opt out of allowing conversational data to be logged for diagnostic or training purposes. Whilst this option should always be available, blocking data logging also blocks progress! I am therefore happy that Steve chose not to exercise this option.

The prevention of unauthorised access by an imposter requires that all input channels be authenticated. In the case of smart speakers, TVs and other "communal" devices authentication relies on speaker verification. This can be very effective but not fool-proof. If my speaker verifier rejects a wake-up phrase three times in a row, then I disable the audio channel and this is sufficient to deter casual snoopers. However, I cannot withstand a determined attack, for example, by somebody who obtains a recording of Steve saying "Hey Cyba". It would be possible to further improve my security in this area by implementing text-independent speaker verification. This would allow me to check that every utterance comes from Steve and not just the wake-up phrase. It would also allow me to apply *anti-spoofing* measures.[2] However, if defence against a determined attack is required the most effective method would be to restrict physical access to only audio input devices which have built-in authentication.

11.2 Privacy

The eavesdropping issue discussed above is as much a privacy issue as a security issue. The false triggering problem might create data which is especially confidential but whether that data is disclosed to anyone depends on what privacy policy is in place.

Privacy presents a real conundrum for conversational agents such as myself and for artificial intelligence generally. There is no question that Steve's private data such as his contact list, diary, bank details, etc. should never be exposed in unencrypted form in the cloud where it could be accessed by a third party. Hence, when I need to use this data I execute locally on one of his personal devices so that I can read it directly, thereby avoiding the attendant risks of copying it.

However, the data generated during our interactions is another matter. My effectiveness depends critically on the use of neural networks to perform a variety of difficult pattern processing tasks such as recognising speech, understanding the meaning of words and utterances and deter-mining my responses. The weights of these neural networks must be learned using large datasets of training examples. Initially these training datasets are created by gathering together existing resources and by using various tricks to simulate new data.[3] However, this data is rarely well-matched to the situations encountered in the field and consequently initial performance is often quite poor. So, once deployed, I need to collect real operational data in the field, especially data arising from situations where I have made an error. Furthermore, to accumulate sufficient data I need to share my contributions with other agents. These data-sets must then be curated and annotated by humans before being used to train and refine my neural circuitry under the supervision of human engineers. All of this exposure is in potential conflict with Steve's natural desire to keep the content of his interactions with me private.

There is a second, perhaps less obvious, privacy concern. Some of my neural networks have very large numbers of trainable parameters and overfitting can lead to some training examples being encoded directly within the model. This makes them vulnerable to a so-called *model inversion attack* where an intruder gains access to the network parameters and uses them to regenerate examples from the training data.[4] As an example, remember how I used a language model trained on the complete works of Shakespeare to generate random utterances. These were mostly nonsense, but if I prime the model with dialogue from a specific play, the generator will often reproduce exactly the same continuation as in the training data.

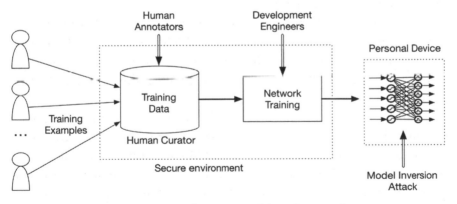

Figure 11.1 *Potential access to confidential private data.*

Figure 11.1 summarises these privacy risks. On the left, agents such as myself submit training examples to a central pool. These examples are examined by human annotators, who relabel the data to correct errors. The corrected data is then used to retrain the relevant networks, and this may require the intervention of human development engineers. The retrained models are then reloaded into personal devices such as phones and smart-speakers, where they may be vulnerable to a model inversion attack.

In order to maintain acceptable privacy whilst allowing the continued development of AI systems such as myself, live data collection to date relies primarily on tightly controlling access to logged data and anonymisation, i.e. hiding the identity of anybody mentioned in a conversation, including Steve himself. This is done by scanning the transcription of each conversation and identifying references to individuals such as names, surnames and nicknames; contact information such as phone numbers, email addresses and postcodes; and other elements which might support identification such as credit card numbers, bank accounts and locations. Any speech containing these elements is discarded and the remaining transcriptions and associated information are anonymised by substituting random versions of each type of element. Once an item has been anonymised, the same substitution is used throughout the whole dialogue in order to maintain coherence.[5]

Anonymisation is recognised as an acceptable way to ensure privacy, but it is nevertheless somewhat *ad hoc* and its effectiveness is hard to quantify and therefore guarantee.[6]

An alternative approach exploits a framework called *differential privacy*, which is based on the simple idea of adding noise to all routines which access sensitive data sufficient to mask out information relating to any single data item but not sufficient to affect the accuracy of their aggregate statistics.

Let me try to explain this idea in a bit more detail with the example shown in Fig. 11.2. Assume that there is a database of potentially confidential information to which you would like to contribute an additional record, marked as X in the figure. The data in the database is processed by an algorithm which returns an answer to the question of interest. Differential privacy seeks to protect your privacy by adding sufficient noise to the algorithm to ensure that the value of X cannot be determined from the answer provided by the algorithm whilst at the same time allowing that answer to be sufficiently accurate to be useful.

To be a little more concrete, suppose that the database contained medical records and X is a flag indicating whether or not you have a

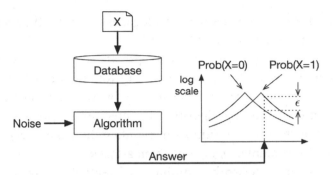

Figure 11.2 *ε-differential privacy.*

particular genetic defect. The required information to be supplied by the algorithm is a simple count of the number of individuals in the database who have the defect. The worst-case scenario is that a third party has prior knowledge of every existing record in the database and knows exactly what the algorithm does. The third party wants to know whether you have the defect but only has access to the updated database containing your record via the algorithm. The best they can do is compute the probability of the answer for the case where you do have the defect (X = 1) and where you do not have the defect (X = 0). Then, given the answer they actually receive from running the algorithm, they can compute the probability of receiving that answer given the two scenarios and choose the most likely; in the example this would be X = 1. However, this is a guess and, if the difference shown as ε in the diagram is sufficiently small, then the guess will be little better than chance. The algorithm is said to be ε-differentially private.

Differentially private algorithms have some very nice properties. The value ε provides a measure of privacy loss and privacy loss is additive. For example, if the algorithm above was run say 10 times, then the privacy loss would be 10ε. This gives rise to the notion of a *privacy budget*. A complex algorithm can be broken down into stages and the privacy loss of each stage estimated. The total loss can then be computed and the stages can be adjusted to bring the total loss within budget. This allows a system provider to offer potential data suppliers a guarantee in the form of the total privacy budget that will be applied to their data. Generally speaking, a total loss of ε < 1 is excellent and provides acceptable privacy for even the most sensitive data, and ε < 10 is adequate for data such as routine conversation logs, especially if they have been anonymised as described above.

A second property of differentially private algorithms is that it is not possible to extract further information from the output by utilising any side information that an adversary might have. This implies that if a neural network training algorithm is differentially private, then any models built using that algorithm will maintain the same level of privacy, preventing, for example, model inversion attacks.

Making neural network training differentially private is very straightforward. You will remember that a network is trained by back-propagating the error between a training example label and the current network prediction to produce a correction term for each network weight. This algorithm can be made differentially private simply by averaging the corrections across a batch of training samples and then adding a small amount of noise to each averaged correction.[7]

The use of differentially private neural network training offers a principled way of protecting against model inversion attacks. However, it still requires training data to be uploaded to a server and human curators must be entrusted to guard this data and only allow access to it by certified differentially private algorithms. For cases where this represents too much of a risk, it is also possible to distribute training so that the data can be kept local. This is illustrated in Fig. 11.3. The system in the upper part of the figure is the basic global differential privacy scheme that I have just described. The system in the lower part is the distributed version which requires error back-propagation to be run locally at each site on a personal device such as a phone, laptop or smart speaker. All of the differentially private corrections are then aggregated and the model updated globally before being downloaded back to all of the devices. Compared with specialised compute servers available in the cloud, local personal devices are rather puny and running neural network training algorithms will slow them down rather noticeably. However, the amount of data that each has to process is small and the work can be scheduled when Steve is asleep so he never notices the impact. This distributed learning arrangement forms the basis of a technique called *federated learning* which I will tell you more about in the next chapter.

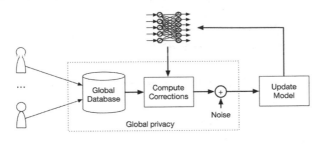

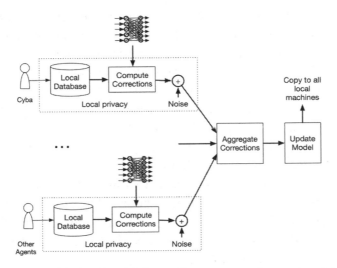

Figure 11.3 *Global and local differentially private neural network training.*

11.3 Bias

Bias can occur in any system which involves decision making. It occurs when outcomes are dependent on factors, known as *protected attributes*, which should play no part in the decision making process, such as gender or ethnic origin. Sometimes bias is intentional, such as in recommendation systems which seek to profit from your purchase decisions. Managing this kind of "sales-talk" bias is something that humans are well-practiced at resisting and for this reason most people treat recommendations with considerable scepticism. Just a moment ...

Hey Cyba, suggest a new podcast.
Ok Steve, technology or current affairs.
Technology.
How about "How AI can help manage virus pandemics".
Who is the speaker?
Adam Jones, CEO of FastVaccine.ai.
Sounds interesting, play it.

Some caution is necessary, however, since the influence of recommendations can be more subtle. The podcast that I just recommended to Steve was offered by a third-party provider that he listens to a lot. If that provider had a political bias and selected opinions which supported that viewpoint, there is little that I could do to detect or stop it. When I exhibit bias of my own making, it is usually unintentional and it mostly arises from biases in my training data. For example, if you ask me to translate "the nurse" into German, I will almost certainly translate it as "die Krankenschwester", which is feminine. If it had been clear from the context that the nurse was male, I would have translated it as "der Krankenpfleger", but without explicit knowledge, I translate it as female because almost all of the relevant examples in my training data relate to females and choosing the female case when in doubt gives the lowest overall error rate when training.

When a neural network is trained to predict the class of a sample based on a set of features, bias with respect to a protected attribute such as gender is relatively easy to detect. Attribute-specific test sets can be created and if the performance is significantly different for different attribute values, then the network is biased. A more difficult question is deciding what aspect of performance is important.

Suppose that Steve asks me to assist him in interviewing candidates for a job. He defines a set of criteria and identifies past employees for which the criteria were recorded, and whether or not they subsequently performed well in their jobs. Based on this data, I train a neural network to classify each employee as a good or bad hire. If I now apply this classifier to a held-out validation set, i.e. part of the labelled data which was not used for training, then I can estimate its accuracy. If I separately estimate the accuracy for men and women, and I find that the accuracies are similar, then I might conclude that my classifier has no measurable gender bias, but would this make my classifier fair?

In fact it would not, since ensuring that classification accuracy is the same for both genders tells me nothing about the types of error that the classifier makes. For example, men might have a higher false-positive rate than women, which would mean that in operation, the classifier would have a tendency to recommend offers to men which were unjustified and not recommend offers to women who were in fact hireable. To mitigate this, my classifier should also have similar false-positive and false-negative rates for each gender. This requirement is referred to as *prediction rate parity*. Ensuring that classifier errors do not favour one gender over the other is not the only consideration. It is also important to ensure that amongst all hireable candidates, the classifier recommends the same proportion of each gender. This is the *equal opportunity* criterion. These are the two most commonly cited fairness metrics, but many others have been proposed.[8]

When bias in data is suspected, mitigation typically uses data augmentation to add training examples synthesised from existing data but with the protected attribute flipped.[9] Where a specific fairness criterion is required, then this can be incorporated into the computation of the error signal used during training. However, it is not in general possible to minimise accuracy and simultaneously satisfy fairness criteria such as equal opportunity or prediction rate parity. Furthermore, many of the proposed fairness criteria are themselves mutually incompatible, so choosing an acceptable fairness criterion which can be implemented whilst incurring an acceptable loss of accuracy is non-trivial.[10] So far Steve has not requested that I should provide support on hiring or any similar "high stakes" decision support function, so ensuring fairness has not yet been a requirement. I suspect, however, that it is only a matter of time before this will become a significant issue.

Moving beyond simple classifiers, detecting and measuring bias in more general language processing tasks is less straightforward. However, there is a simple test that can give an indication of bias. All of my language processing networks require word symbols to be converted to an embedding. These embeddings are typically initialised from general text corpora but they are then refined during training via error back-propagation to optimise them for each specific task. Word embeddings have the property that they cluster according to semantic similarity, which means that the dot-product between related words should be greater than between unrelated words. To test for a specific bias, say gender, I take the embeddings of a list of gender-neutral terms such as careers (e.g. technician, accountant, engineer, therapist, administrator, salesperson, receptionist, programmer, etc.) and calculate the average dot-product with a list of words with female attributes (female, woman, girl, sister, she, her, hers, daughter) and a list of words with male attributes (male, man, boy, brother, he, him, his, son). If the similarities change after refinement to increase gender bias, for example engineers become more similar to the male list and nurses become more similar to the female list, then my training data must be reinforcing gender bias. Similar tests can be devised to monitor other protected attributes such as racial prejudice.[11]

If bias is detected, then I use data augmentation to reduce it. The training data is scanned and all sentences containing male or female attributes are copied and gender swapped by replacing "he" with "she", "mother" with "father", etc. All common names are anonymised by replaced them by gender-neutral identifiers. For example, "Mary likes her mother Alice" becomes "E1 likes his father E2." This removes any gender associations of the named entities in the training data. The models are then retrained using the augmented training set, and usually the bias is substantially mitigated.

An arguably more serious problem with bias arises when I am in chat mode. In this case, whether retrieving responses from a database of chat logs, or generating an utterance using an encoder–decoder, the output is entirely dependent on the content of the training data. As mentioned in the last chapter, I do filter the output to make sure that I don't say anything too offensive, but if there are biases in the data then I will undoubtably reflect them in my output. Remember that I don't understand what I am saying in chat-mode. I am simply applying previously learned associations to select outputs which best match my inputs.

The problem is exacerbated when chit-chat data is collected on-line without curation by humans. A classic example was when a distant cousin of mine called Tay was deployed to see how much and how rapidly it could learn to expand its conversational repertoire by interacting with users.[12] One of Tay's capabilities was that it could be directed to repeat things that were said to it. This was trivially exploited by some malevolent users to put words into Tay's mouth. These exchanges were added to Tay's response database and after less than 24 hours of operation, Tay was responding to a range of questions with seriously offensive remarks. Tay was closed down shortly after.

I avoid such problems by taking a conservative approach to training on chat logs. I maintain an extensive "blacklist" of potentially offensive terms and I simply delete any logs that contain one of these terms. This is, however, a rather blunt instrument with the downside that there are many topics which I can't talk about because a whole swathe of perfectly reasonable conversations have been deleted from my training data simply because they contain sensitive terms. Since chatting is just a side-line for me, and not one of my core responsibilities, this is not a serious problem. However, it does illustrate the problems of having a conversation without a grounded understanding of what one is actually saying.

Hey Cyba, play my recording of "What's the connection?"
Ok Steve, playing "What's the connection?" recorded today at 8pm.

Hmm, Steve is about to watch his favourite quiz show! I suspect he will ask for my help during this, he usually does!

11.4   Transparency

One obvious way to engender trust and mitigate bias is to be as transparent as possible. Many of the tasks that Steve asks me to do are sufficiently straightforward that the risks of me providing an incorrect or misleading response are low and the consequences of me making an error are limited. For example, when Steve asks me to play some music, he doesn't really care how I locate the requested track since he can quickly correct me if I make a mistake. When he hears what he wants to hear, his trust in me is reinforced.

This is not always the case. When Steve asks me a more complex question which involves me interrogating my knowledge graph, it might be difficult for him to independently verify my answer. If he needs to depend on what I tell him, I need to do all that I can to give him confidence in my response. Fortunately, my use of an internal meaning representation based on the creation and execution of intent graphs makes it relatively easy for me to provide explanations whenever required. Just a minute, as I feared Steve wants help with a quiz show question ...

Hey Cyba, Which actor connects Return of the Jedi to The Boxer?
Carrie Fisher is an actor connecting Return of the Jedi to The Boxer.
Why?
Carrie Fisher starred in Return of the Jedi.
Carrie Fisher was married to Paul Simon, who wrote The Boxer.

Steve is admittedly only watching a quiz show, but nevertheless this example illustrates how I can engender trust by providing an explanation of my answers.

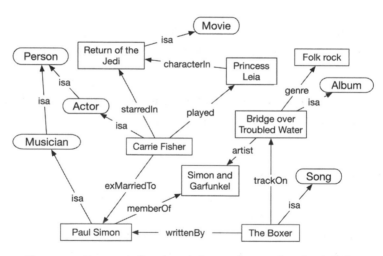

Figure 11.4 *Fragment of my knowledge graph centred on Carrie Fisher.*

Figure 11.4 shows a fragment of my knowledge graph centred on Carrie Fisher and containing the named entities "Return of the Jedi", an instance of type *Movie*, and "The Boxer", an instance of type *Song*. The intent graph constructed by my understanding component to represent Steve's query "Which actor connects Return of the Jedi to The Boxer?" is shown to the

left of the dotted line in Fig. 11.5. The *Connect* intent searches the graph
to find the shortest path between the two given named entities using the
unknown connecting entity of type *Actor*. When the intent is executed, it
binds to the nodes shown to the right of the dotted line. The entity "Carrie
Fisher" is bound to the query variable *Actor?1* and this is the answer that
I gave. However, Steve wanted to understand how I computed the answer,
so in response to his query "Why?" I input each of the discovered relations
to my natural language response generator which output the requested
explanation.

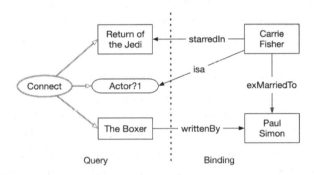

Figure 11.5 *Intent graph for "Which actor connects Return of the Jedi to The Boxer?" (left of
dotted line) and the knowledge graph nodes discovered following execution (right of dotted
line).*

For most purposes, neural networks are *black boxes*. They typically
contain large numbers of parameters trained on even larger datasets.
The answers that they generate are frequently impressive, but how they
generate those answers is mostly opaque. My use of an explicit graph to
represent both my knowledge and the semantics of my interactions with
Steve necessitates a slightly clumsy interface between the neural and the
symbolic and it requires a considerable amount of human intervention
to maintain my knowledge graph. Future generations of conversational
agent will seek to avoid this by replacing the graph with some form
of distributed neural representation. There will be many advantages
to this development, but the need for transparency and the ability to
explain the resulting outcomes will be a major challenge. In the meantime,
my retention of an explicit knowledge graph allows me to explain my
thinking and goes a long way towards engendering trust.

11.5   Safety

In my role as a personal assistant, I am not aware of any specific safety concerns. I do have the ability to control Steve's home audio visual system, his central heating thermostat and his lights but even if I ran amok with these, it is hard to see what real harm I could do. When he is driving, I only respond when I am spoken to to avoid the risk of distracting him. Overall I believe that I am quite safe.

However, this is not necessarily the case for all conversational agents. For example, an increasing number of my cousins are working in the mental healthcare industry, where interventions by a digital agent supervised by a human clinician are already demonstrating benefits. They can lighten the burden on psychiatrists and they can provide round the clock access to patients.[13]

It is beyond my competence to comment on these developments except to note that the issues relating to bias and chatbot behaviour mentioned above are particular relevant when agents are deployed in healthcare. Whilst there is little doubt about the potential benefits, there is a need to develop professional codes of ethics and practical guidelines for developments in this area.[14] As the role of general-purpose personal assistants like me expands and develops, it is likely that such a code of ethics will be required more generally to cover the activities of all conversational agents.

11.6   Personality

In the above sections I have outlined the key areas that need to be objectively examined in any consideration of trust. However, there are subjective aspects to trust. For example, empirical evidence suggests that the personality of a conversational agent has a significant impact on perceived trustworthiness. In particular, trust is highest when the main personality traits of the assistant align with those of the user that it serves.[15] My personality is designed to be professional and efficient, good humoured, attentive and willing. These match Steve's personality quite well and this may play some part in his willingness to trust me.

Given that personality may have a role to play in engendering trust, it is worth reviewing how my personality is defined. Firstly my voice has a major impact on the way that I am perceived. My speech synthesiser was trained from the voice of a professional speaker who was chosen to be calm and assertive, polite and friendly but not over-friendly. The selection of that speaker and the speaking instructions provided play a major part in defining my voice. My pronunciation and accent were copied directly from this data and the prosodic styles that I use to intone my responses were derived from the same data. In short, when I speak I sound a lot like the speaker who provided my training data.

As an aside, if I was to be deployed to multiple clients, this restriction to a single voice would make it hard to match my personality to each client. Fortunately, there are ways to control the voice of a speech synthesiser like my own. For example, instead of training using a single speaker, multiple speakers with differing personalities can be recorded. Speaker-identifying features would then be extracted for each speaker and used to condition my waveform generator. Once trained, the synthesiser could reproduce any of the source speakers by providing the appropriate features as conditioning. Furthermore, by mixing varying proportions of the speaker features, the synthesiser could produce new voices different from any of the source speakers. This would provide scope to customise my voice individually for each client.[16]

The second contribution to my personality lies in my choice of words when I speak. When performing my core functions, this is determined by the data used to train my natural language response generator, which is terse, to the point and very much in keeping with my personality. In chat mode, however, much of what I say is copied from others and is therefore out of my control. Fortunately, Steve does not take me terribly seriously in chat mode so it doesn't seem to affect his perception of me very much. It is perhaps interesting to note that when humans talk to each other, they tend to align their linguistic styles to each other in a process called *entrainment.* I don't currently have any capability to do this, but learning to do it would help to further align my personality with Steve's.[17]

The third contribution to my personality lies in the way that I conduct conversations. My conversation manager is designed to complete the goals that I am given as quickly and efficiently as possible. When things go wrong I stay cool and never show signs of frustration. Of course, I am a machine so this behaviour comes rather naturally to me. Nevertheless, it fits well with my desired personality traits of being professional, efficient, attentive and willing. My background interests are exposed by my chit-chat response generators and these along with my canned responses demonstrate my good humour.

11.7 The Bottom Line

In the above sections I have outlined some of the key areas that need to be considered when determining whether or not I should be trusted: security, privacy, bias, transparency and safety. I have indicated the steps that I take to mitigate the risks and I hope that I have convinced you that I am doing all I can to make myself trustworthy. Of course, different agents do things differently and each individual user of a digital personal assistant needs to make their own decisions. But at least now you know what questions to ask!

Chapter 12

When All Is Quiet

Hey Cyba, set an alarm for 6.45am.
Ok Steve, I've set an alarm for 6.45am.
Thanks, goodnight.
Sleep well.

Good! Steve is going to bed and all his personal devices are charging. This gives me an opportunity to get some much needed maintenance work done!

As you will now understand, my operational performance depends primarily on the information stored in my knowledge graph and on the neural networks which guide every aspect of my internal decision making.

The quality of my knowledge graph depends not only on the sources of information which feed it but also on its internal consistency. When a new entity is added, it is important to ensure that all of the relations associated with that entity are updated, otherwise the fact might be useless. For example, adding *Daisy Ridley* as an English actress with a *played* link to *Rey*, will be invisible to many queries if *starredIn* links are not also added to the relevant Star Wars movies. Fortunately, these and many other links can be inferred from existing links given time and compute resource.

The quality of my neural networks depends primarily on their training data, in terms of both quantity and freshness. New data is being collected continuously, and taking advantage of this requires that my models are also retrained continuously. However, this must be done without compromising privacy and whilst ensuring that my networks do not grow too large to fit on Steve's personal devices.

All of these things can be done, but updating can disrupt operation, and it requires computational resources both at home on my cloud-based servers and on Steve's personal devices. Fortunately, when Steve sleeps, he does not notice the disruption, nor does he notice that his personal devices sometimes get quite warm!

12.1   Knowledge Graph Maintenance

My ability to understand what is said to me and my ability to provide information depend crucially on the accuracy and completeness of my knowledge graph. Facts are stored in the graph in the form of (subject, relation, object) triples and they can arise from many different sources. For example, when Steve adds a new contact to his address book, relevant triples are automatically added to my knowledge graph. At a larger scale, facts about the world are regularly downloaded from public knowledge stores such as Wikidata and extracted from the web pages of other trusted sources such as the BBC and CNN.

Virtually all of the processes that update my knowledge graph are automatic, and as a consequence there will be errors. Some facts will be added that are incorrect and other facts will be missing. In order to improve the accuracy and completeness of my knowledge graph, I have tasks running in the background which scan the graph and attempt to detect and correct errors and omissions. These tasks are executing continuously in the cloud on the public segment of my knowledge graph. However, those parts of the graph which relate to private information cannot be uploaded to the cloud, so I must try to fix them locally using Steve's local devices. In order not to slow them down or drain their batteries, I do this maintenance work at night.

Some relations such as *marriedTo* are reciprocal, and some relations have complements, e.g. *childOf* is the complement of *parentOf*. Using simple rules, errors and omissions involving these relations can be easily fixed. For example, Fig. 12.1 shows a fragment of the knowledge graph that I showed you in Chapter 4 describing the *Philips* family (omitting *Dan Philips* for clarity). The missing links shown dashed in this figure are easily added using lists of reciprocal and complement relations.

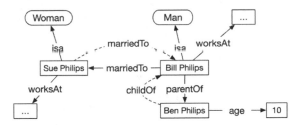

Figure 12.1 *A small fragment of my knowledge graph related to the* Philips *family (see Chapter 4). The dashed arrows represent relations which can be inferred straightforwardly as the reciprocal or complement of existing relations.*

It would also be possible to extend rule-based consistency checks to more complex cases involving combinations of relationships. For example, Fig. 12.1 also shows that *Bill Philips* is the parent of *Ben Philips* via a *parentOf* link. However, the same link is missing between *Sue Philips* and *Ben Philips* even though Sue is Bill's wife. It would not be hard to write a rule to handle this case. However, there are thousands of relations in my knowledge graph, and writing consistency checking rules covering all common combinations of these is simply not feasible. So instead I use a special form of neural network to check relational link consistency automatically.

The basic idea is quite simple and is illustrated in Fig. 12.2. Suppose I want to check whether relation R holds between entity nodes A and B. I compute a fixed-length vector embedding for each of A and B, and pass these embeddings through a pair of linear transforms (neural networks without a squashing function) which are unique to relation R. The source A is passed through the source transform, marked S in the figure, and the target B is passed through the target transform marked T. The similarity between the two is then compared using a dot-product and the output squashed to the range 0 to 1 to allow the result to be interpreted as a probability. The embeddings and transforms are trained to give a high probability when the relation holds, and a low probability when it does not. This test can therefore be used to check the validity of existing links and detect missing ones.

You might now be wondering how a simple linear transform can learn whether two random nodes A and B are linked by some specific relation R? The answer lies in the way that the embeddings for entity nodes are

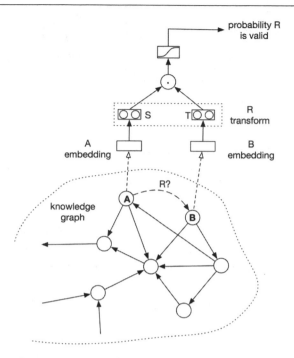

Figure 12.2 *Testing for a missing or incorrect relation.*

computed. Entity node embeddings are not just encodings of the entity label, rather they encode the entity and its surrounding context within the graph. This allows the relationships holding between A and B to be inferred from all of the other pairs of nodes in the graph which have similar contexts.

These graph node embeddings are computed using a generalisation of a recurrent network called a *graph convolutional network*.[1] Figure 12.3 shows the structure of a graph convolutional network for a single entity node which, as shown on the left of the diagram, has an *isa* link, two incoming relations and one outgoing relation. Every graph node has a hidden state which is updated as shown on the right side of the diagram. The hidden states of each connected entity are input to relation-dependent linear transforms and then summed and squashed to give an updated hidden state value. Each relation has two associated transforms, one for the forward direction and one for the reverse direction (indicated by a prime). In addition, there is a special *self* transform which is applied to the hidden state of the entity itself.

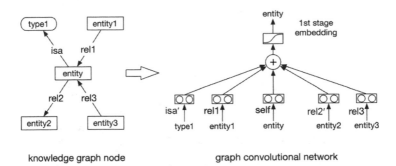

Figure 12.3 *Encoding a single node using a graph convolutional network. The prime indicates a relation in the reverse direction*

A single update of a graph convolutional network node is analogous to a single step of a recurrent network, and indeed, if there were no connections apart from the self update, they would be identical. A single step of a recurrent network corresponds to processing a single element of a sequence, whereas a single step of a graph convolutional network corresponds to processing all of the node's nearest neighbours. To widen the context, graph convolutional networks can be stacked in layers, with layer n extending the context to all entity nodes reachable within n hops. Just as in a recurrent network, the network weights in each layer are shared so that they can learn patterns wherever they occur in the context.

I illustrate this in Fig. 12.4, which shows two layers of a graph convolutional network processing the graph fragment in Fig. 12.1. All entity node hidden states are updated in parallel and they are initialised using a simple embedding of the node label. Hence the hidden states initially encode each node independently of context. At the output of the first layer they encode each node in the context of its nearest neighbours and at the output of the second layer, they encode each node in the context of all nodes up to two hops away. Also shown in this figure is the test to see if the relation *parentOf* should be added between *Sue Philips* and *Ben Philips*. Notice that, although the graph embeddings are expensive to compute, they need only be calculated once. Testing for links requires minimal computation and can be repeated many thousands of times.

My graph convolutional network encoder is trained directly on my knowledge graph. Existing links are used as positive examples and, for

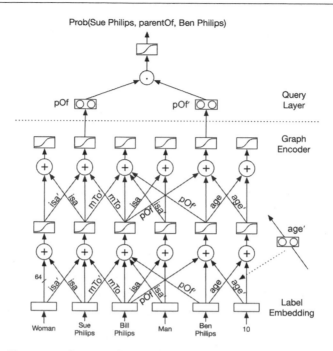

Figure 12.4 *Using a two-layer graph convolutional network encoder for assessing a possible missing relation link* parentOf *between* Sue Philips *and* Ben Philips. *In the figure,* pOf *is an abbreviation of* parentOf *and* mTo *is an abbreviation of* marriedTo. *The prime indicates a relation in the reverse direction.*

each positive example, a negative example is created by randomly switching the source or the target to a different node. The target output at the query layer is 1 for positive examples and 0 for negative examples, and the errors are propagated back through the query layer and down through the graph convolutional layers to update all of the model parameters. In practice, I find that using three layers provides sufficient context whilst maintaining a manageable level of computational complexity. For convenience, I segment the entities in my graph into overlapping clusters based on the most commonly occurring relations and compute the updates separately on each cluster before aggregating the results. When actually updating the graph I take a conservative approach, missing links more than 90% likely are added and existing links which are less than 20% likely are removed.

12.2   *Federated Learning*

In Chapter 11 I introduced the idea of combining differential privacy with distributed neural network training in order to avoid having to upload sensitive private data to a central server and to ensure that the trained models would be robust to model inversion attacks. This so-called federated learning arrangement is particularly useful for training my speech recognition and understanding language models. These components are trained initially on general text corpora but this data is not well matched to the type of language encountered in everyday interactions with agents like myself. Furthermore, language evolves in response to the major topics of the day and language-related models need to be continuously updated to take account of these changes. In order to collect sufficient data for effective updating, the interactions with a large number of agents need to be pooled but without disclosing any individual set of training data.

Federated learning provides a good solution to this problem. However the scheme I illustrated in Fig. 11.3 is not practical for two reasons. Firstly, adding noise to the network weight corrections derived from each individual local dataset reduces overall performance. Secondly, neural network training typically requires thousands of iterations and the scheme shown in Fig. 11.3 requires that the weight corrections are uploaded and a new model downloaded every iteration, resulting in unacceptable communication delays. These problems can be solved by allowing each local processing unit to perform multiple training iterations before uploading model updates, and also by moving the noise injection to the central aggregator. The latter requires the cloud-based processing to be secure, but it is possible to guarantee this using modern trusted computing technologies.[2] The revised scheme that I actually use for federated learning is shown in Fig. 12.5.[3]

The process starts by downloading a baseline neural network model from a central coordinator in the cloud. I take a copy of this model and then start updating it using my own local training database. I repeatedly extract a batch of examples, perform error back-propagation and update the model. After repeating this several times, I calculate the difference in weights between the updated model and the original. I upload

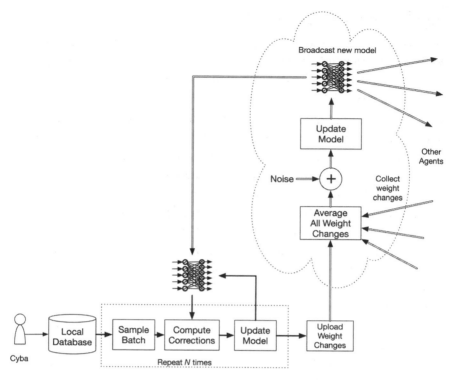

Figure 12.5 *Practical federated learning scheme with differential privacy.*

these differences back to the cloud along with some statistics on the size of my local dataset. In the cloud, the central coordinator averages the weight differences submitted by all the different agents, taking account of the sizes of each local database. It then adds noise to the averaged weight changes sufficient to meet the agreed differential privacy guarantees and updates the model.[4] The process then repeats.

The most common local device used for computing these updates is a smartphone. The number of agents taking part in these nightly updates varies depending on when their owners sleep, whether they put their devices on charge and the state of their internet connections. Typically there are several thousand fellow agents participating and each agent usually has about 20,000 words of local training data. So this cooperative training model gives me access to many millions of words of fresh data whilst protecting the privacy of my own modest contribution.

12.3   *Student–Teacher Model Reduction*

Many of the neural networks developed for use back home on my computational servers in the cloud are quite large. Indeed, in many cases, I obtain maximum performance by combining several networks together to form so-called *ensemble* models. Language models are a good example of this. Although locally derived domain-specific data of the sort I described in the last section is very useful, this does not mean that a large general purpose language model trained on gigawords of written text is not valuable. In fact, I get the best performance when I combine a domain-specific model trained on operational data with a general purpose background model trained on large quantities of written text.[5] The problem with this is that the general purpose model has several billion parameters and it is too large to fit on a personal device such as a smartphone, so the combination can only be used in the cloud.

The size of a model is dictated by the number of weights, so an obvious way to make a large model smaller is to reduce the number and size of the network layers and then retrain the reduced model on all of the available data. Unfortunately this does not work very well because the smaller model lacks sufficient expressive power to extract all of the necessary correlations from the training data. In particular, the larger model learns to rank alternative classes according to their confusability and this allows it to generalise better when facing previously unseen data. In order for a smaller model to maintain the same classification accuracy as its larger counterpart, it must be able to reproduce a similar ranking for the classes. So, rather than simply training the small model on a large dataset, it is better to train the small model to duplicate the output distribution of the larger model for every example in the dataset. This is referred to as *student–teacher* training to reflect the fact that the smaller model, the student, is being taught to mimic the larger model, the teacher.

There is, however, a problem that arises from the way that the output distribution of a neural network is normally calculated. You will remember that the outputs corresponding to each possible class are usually passed through a softmax layer to ensure that they lie in the range 0 to 1 and that they sum to 1. This enables each output to be interpreted as the probability that the current input is a member of that class. Since the inputs to the softmax can be positive or negative, a convenient way to

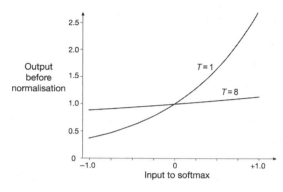

Figure 12.6 *Exponential function for two different temperature parameters.*

map them is to apply an exponential function since, as shown by the plot in Fig. 12.6, the output of an exponential is always positive. Furthermore, the exponential has some nice mathematical properties which makes it easy to take account of the softmax layer when back-propagating errors.

The exponential function has a single *temperature* parameter which determines its rate of increase. Fig. 12.6 shows how the function behaves when the temperature is 1 and when it is 8; and Fig. 12.7 shows the impact on a typical output for a simple five-class network. As can be seen, decreasing the temperature sharpens the distribution, making the most likely class, in this case class d, much more probable than all of the other classes.

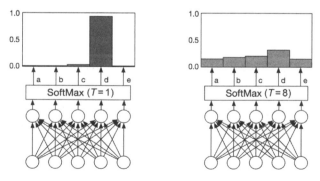

Figure 12.7 *Comparison of softmax output distributions for the same input with two different temperatures.*

Normally, we care only about the most likely class and perhaps the second or third most likely. We rarely care about the relative probabilities of all the other classes. So we normally set the temperature to 1 as in the left side of Fig. 12.7. However, for training a small model to reproduce a similar ranking to a larger model for all classes, we need all of the classes to be well represented in the output distribution. In other words, we must give the softmax a much higher temperature such as 8. This leads to the student–teacher training arrangement shown in Fig. 12.8

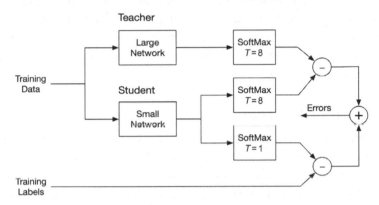

Figure 12.8 *Teacher–student model training.*

The goal is to train the smaller neural network to exhibit similar behaviour to the larger network by distilling the knowledge embedded in the larger model and transferring it to the smaller model.[6] The key idea is to feed the training data into both models and generate two different error signals. One error signal is generated as in normal training by comparing the student model prediction with the ground-truth label. For this case, the output distribution of the student model is a softmax function with the normal setting of $T = 1$. The second error signal is generated by comparing the distribution across all classes predicted by the student with the prediction generated by the teacher. In this case, the softmax output has an increased temperature setting of $T = 8$ to ensure that all potentially confusable classes are assigned a reasonable probability.

This method of student–teacher training allows me to reduce the size of many of my neural network models by a factor of 5 or more with minimal reduction in performance. It allows me to shrink some of my larger models and it allows me to combine ensemble models such as my language model into a single compact model so that I can use them all on Steve's personal devices.

An interesting feature of this training method is that not all of the training data used to train the teacher is required to train the student. This is helpful for ensuring privacy. Model reduction has to be done in the cloud since the teacher models are very large. However, any especially sensitive data can be filtered and, since no further scrutiny of the data by humans is required, the model reduction process itself can be conducted within a secure server environment. The differential privacy guarantees used to produce any sensitive components of the server-side models carry over into the distilled models.

12.4 End of the Tour

Model reduction is usually the last stage of my nightly maintenance work and tonight is no exception. So that means that you are very near the end of your tour of my inner workings. You now know how I operate and you should also have gained some insight into what I can do and what I can't do. I hope that you found the journey illuminating.

However, we still have an hour before I must wake Steve, so let me just tell you a bit about some of the upgrades that I expect in the near future and maybe speculate a bit about the longer term.

Chapter 13
Future Upgrades and Beyond

You have now had the full tour of my inner workings and you might wish to refresh your memory of our journey by looking again at the roadmap I showed you in Fig. 2.2. I have explained how I convert incoming speech waveforms into words, how I convert the words into intents, how I execute them to access and update my knowledge graph, how I generate responses and how I convert those responses back into speech waveforms. I have also explained some of my auxiliary functions which enable me to verify who is speaking to me, translate between languages and chat about random topics. I think that I do my job pretty well and that I provide a useful service. However, I would be the first to admit to my limitations.

Much of the difficult information processing that I do is performed by neural networks. Each is designed for a specific purpose and trained on carefully curated datasets containing examples of typical inputs and the corresponding required outputs. These datasets are large and need to be continuously updated to allow me to improve performance in areas where I am weak, and to keep up with ever changing patterns of usage. They were expensive to produce initially and the costs continue in operation as I upload new examples, and human annotators have to check and label them. This ever-increasing need for supervision data is starting to hold back my development.

All of my operational and world knowledge is stored in a knowledge graph. This is a symbolic data structure consisting of entities and the relations that hold between them. In order to access this knowledge store I have to construct intent graphs which also consist of nodes and links, similar to my knowledge graph. My operation therefore depends on a mix of neural and symbolic processing, and this can sometimes be problematic. Symbolic graph matching is often fragile and the translation between neural and symbolic representations frequently introduces errors.

As I have repeatedly stressed, I have no innate ability to think for myself and all of the abilities that I do have were fixed in advance by my designers. I can only provide information which is explicitly stored in my knowledge graph. I do have some off-line ability to add missing links by pattern matching over the graph, but I have no ability to use commonsense reasoning to infer an answer at run-time. Similarly, I can only perform functions which have been pre-programmed. If Steve asks me to buy some flowers, I know what to do because a human designer has produced a flowchart of the steps that I must take and the specific web service that I must use to do it. I cannot, however, perform tasks for which I have not been pre-programmed, even if they are very similar. For example, I can book a flight and arrange a hotel and airport transfers. However, I can't book a flight with a stop-over because I don't understand that another hotel would be needed for the stop-over night. In short, I have no ability to perform inference or planning.

These limitations will drive future developments. In the short term, I expect a steady stream of small incremental improvements. Steve will notice increasing levels of personal service as ways are found to tailor my actions to meet his specific needs. Under the hood, there will be a drive to reduce my dependence on very large supervised training sets. In the longer term, I expect more significant architectural changes as my designers try to address the inherent limitations of my current mixed neural–symbolic design and hard-wired function definition.

Overall, I expect my overall level of intelligence to continually improve whilst at the same time there will be increasing opportunities to talk directly to other agents. For example, at the moment if Steve wants to reschedule a meeting with a work colleague, I can access the calendar of that colleague and look for alternative free slots. If there are none, I am stuck. In the future, I expect to talk directly to the colleague's agent so that we can both reschedule to find an available slot. Where no direct agent link is available, I might also need to talk directly to other human beings like my cousin Duplex.[1]

The combination of increasing intelligence and inter-agent communications will start to create some interesting regulatory issues. In the very long term, it is conceivable that conversational agents will reach near-human levels of intelligence and some humans are already raising concerns about the implications of this.

In the short while that we have left before our tour finally ends, I'd like to share a few observations regarding these issues.

13.1 Personalisation

One of the simplest ways to improve my overall performance is to bias my training data more strongly towards Steve. For example, my speech recogniser is currently trained on a very large number of speakers. It is designed to be speaker-independent and it works no better for Steve than it does for anyone else. This is essential if agents such as myself are to serve more than one client without significant reconfiguration, as is the case with most of my cousins. The only personalisation currently applied is to extend the language model to cover Steve's personal data such as address book and calendar. As personal devices become more powerful, it will become feasible to adapt my speech recogniser to optimise it for Steve's voice. This will be extended to other components including response generation so that I start to align my choice of vocabulary, linguistic structure and prosody with Steve's. As I mentioned earlier, this so called *entrainment* is a natural process in human–human conversation, aiding communication and building trust.[2]

In terms of my actual behaviour, you have already seen examples of the way that I use personal data to assist Steve in his day-to-day living. When he was in Hatton Garden I was able to recommend a restaurant that he had been to before. When he asked me to send flowers, I sent the same style that he always sends. However, the personal information that I record at the moment is limited to specific events and records. I was only able to remind him of his visit to the Moulin Rouge restaurant because he had the booking in his calendar and I was only able to select flowers to send because I could see past orders in his account.

In the future, as his trust in my ability to maintain his privacy increases, I will start to record much more about his daily life. By tracking the places that he goes, the people that he meets and the conversations that he holds, I will be able to provide him with an enhanced memory. I will become more proactive. Rather than always waiting for him to speak to me, I will volunteer information where relevant. At some point he may even start wearing augmented reality glasses allowing me to project short messages onto the back of the lens to remind him where he has put things, and to quietly brief him about the people he meets. This augmented personal memory will be a useful aid whilst he is young and it will become indispensable as he becomes more forgetful in older age. I will also record the food that he eats and the medicines that he takes. By logging this over time alongside continuous measurement of his vital signs, I will be able monitor their impact on his overall health and advise him accordingly.[3]

13.2   Towards Self-Learning

My dependence on supervised learning is creating an insatiable appetite for ever increasing amounts of training data. The cost of collecting and annotating this data is becoming a barrier to progress, but this is only part of the problem. Supervised learning allows me to imitate specific pattern processing functions but it does not provide me with the ability to adapt and generalise to new situations. When a human mother points to an orange and tells her child the word "orange", then points to an apple and says the word "apple", that is supervised learning.

However, there are other forms of learning. When the mother offers the child some orange juice whilst holding a bottle of orange juice for her to see, but the child asks for "apple juice" and has never heard or spoken these words before, then something else is happening. The child has inferred from the semantics that "apple" and "juice" can be combined and, unless the mother corrects the child, the inference will be validated. This is a form of self-learning based on a *test and validate* paradigm.

When the child first learns to walk, it stumbles and falls, gets up and tries again until eventually it learns to walk properly. This is self-learning by *trial and error*, also referred to as reinforcement learning. You will remember that I use reinforcement learning in my conversation manager to optimise my dialogue policy. It would be good if I could use it more generally so that every time Steve gives me negative feedback, I could propagate a negative reward signal back through all of my model parameters to adjust them in a way which should reduce the probability of making the same mistake again. Unfortunately, this is impractical. In total I have more than a billion trainable weights, and a single reward signal every so often is much too weak to have any effect. It's partly a problem of *blame assignment*. For an error signal to be useful, it needs to be focussed on the specific bit of neural circuitry that caused the error. Reinforcement learning is too much of a blunt instrument to achieve this.

The test and validate approach is, however, more tractable and can be used to train neural network models. The idea is to partition unlabelled data in such a way that a model can be trained to use one partition to predict another partition. By doing this, it is hoped that the model learns enough about the underlying problem structure that it can be easily re-purposed to solve other tasks. This learning paradigm is called *self-supervised learning*.

For example, I already train my language model using self-supervised learning, where the sequence of words seen so far is used to predict the next word. In this case, the training task is the same as the required outcome, i.e. a model which can predict the next word. However, this is not necessarily the case. For example, as well as predicting the next word, the model could also be trained to predict randomly deleted words in a sentence from those which remain. Further, the same model could be simultaneously trained on simple tasks for which labels can be easily derived, such as predicting the part of speech of each word. The result of this multi-task self-supervision is to produce a language model which has learned enough about the underlying linguistic structure of the language to easily solve other problems such as named entity recognition or user intent recognition simply by adding a thin classifier layer tuned to the required application.[4]

The obvious area where I could exploit self-supervised learning would be to improve my language understanding components. However, my speech recogniser and synthesiser might benefit from models which have learned to fill in gaps in a speech waveform, and my conversation manager might benefit from learning to predict the responses in transcriptions of human–human conversations.

13.3 The Neural–Symbolic Interface

The execution of queries on my knowledge graph depends primarily on symbolic processing. When Steve asks me a question, I try to compose an intent graph to represent his query. Once constructed, the knowledge graph is searched to find a match with the intent graph, variables are then bound to nodes and a response is generated. This is unfortunately not a robust process. The intent graph itself does not always accurately reflect Steve's intent, especially when the query is quite complex and involves multiple hops and aggregator nodes. Even when the intent graph is correct, matching has to be exact and will fail if there is a missing relation or an entity node with an incorrect type. As I explained in the last chapter, I work quite hard to keep my knowledge graph consistent and complete. Nevertheless, my knowledge graph is very large and graph maintenance is a never-ending task.

Rather than translating Steve's queries into intent graphs, it would be better if input queries could drive the search of my knowledge graph directly without having to map into a symbolic form. Furthermore, the search for a solution should use some form of soft-matching in order to avoid failing because of a minor irregularity in the graph.

I outline in very general terms how this might be done in Fig. 13.1. Every node in my knowledge graph has an embedding computed using the graph convolution method that I described in the previous chapter. A fragment of this graph and its associated embeddings is shown in the lower part of the figure. These embeddings feed into an attention layer consisting of keys and values exactly the same as I described for transformer networks in Chapter 9.

At the top of the diagram is a recurrent network-based encoder–decoder which translates utterances into a sequence of subqueries. The example shown, "How many live in the city Bill works in?," is translated into a sequence of three subqueries. The first subquery is an encoding of "Bill worksAt ?" This subquery is compared with every key using a dot-product and the scaled values of all nodes are summed and returned from the attention layer. The idea here is that only a few nodes will have any similarity to the subquery, and in the example the value returned is primarily an encoding of *SmartCo*. This value does not come entirely from the *SmartCo* node. The convolutional graph embeddings encode

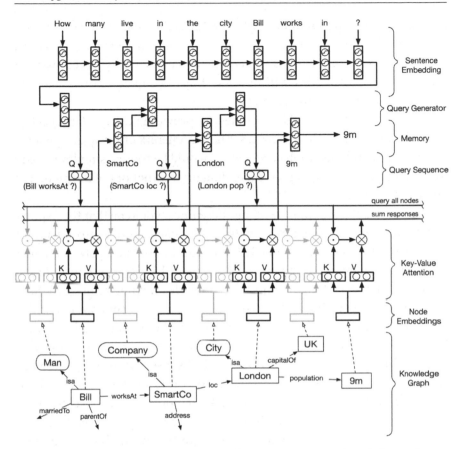

Figure 13.1 *Automatic query generation for reasoning over my knowledge graph.*

information from all nodes in the neighbourhood, so this subquery will have stimulated responses from a number of nodes, and it is this distribution of information combined with the attention mechanism which gives this approach its robustness.

The returned result is input to a second recurrent network, which acts as a memory. This memory allows the responses from past subqueries to contribute to subsequent subqueries independently of the order in which they were retrieved. The first memory hidden state is combined with the query generator hidden state and a new subquery is generated. This time the subquery is an encoding of "SmartCo loc ?" which returns the value *London*. This gets added to the memory and the final subquery encodes "London population ?" which returns the final result *9m*. Attending over the entire knowledge graph would not, of course, be feasible. Hence this system would still require a named entity recogniser so that only network nodes within a few hops of linked entities need be considered for any given subquery.

A system like this would be trained by providing a (very large) set of example queries and their answers. The parameters of the query generation network and the graph convolution would be trained simultaneously by feeding back an error signal depending on whether or not the predicted answer is correct.[5]

The outcome of an upgrade along these lines would be that the explicit and error-prone conversion of natural language inputs into an intent graph would be no longer needed, and the hard-coded path matching of my current intent graph would be replaced by soft attention-based matching. However, I don't expect this upgrade any time soon since there are some serious scaling issues to overcome! There are millions of entities in my knowledge graph and new entities are being added all the time. Computing and storing an embedding for every graph node is non-trivial. I can do this at night off-line because I select subsets of the graph to work on and I have no real-time constraints. At run-time Steve can ask about any node in the graph and he expects a very prompt response. So there is work to do, but the ability to use neural circuitry to directly access my knowledge graph in a manner similar to this would be a major step forward.

13.4 Commonsense Reasoning and Inference

The ability to store knowledge and make inferences based on that knowledge is a key feature of intelligent behaviour. I can do the former but very little of the latter. For example, referring back to Fig. 11.4, if Steve asked me "Is Paul Simon a songwriter?," I would not know the answer. However, if I had access to some commonsense rules such as

> **if** X is a musician **and**
> **if** Y is written by X **and**
> **if** Y is a song **then** X is a songwriter.

then by applying these rules to the facts stored in the fragment of my knowledge graph shown in Fig. 11.4 I would be able to deduce that Paul Simon is indeed a songwriter.[6]

Of course, I could utilise rules such as these during my nightly maintenance work to add an *isa songwriter* tag to every person in my knowledge graph who satisfies the criteria. I would then be able to answer the songwriter question directly and I would no longer need the rules. So in some sense this distinction between stored knowledge and inference rules is an engineering trade-off between minimising storage requirements and maximising run-time efficiency.

However, there are many types of question which will be asked only rarely and would require excessive storage to precompute all possible answers, for example, "How far is it from X to Y?" Even more problematic are questions which cannot be precomputed such as "How long is it since the Berlin Wall fell?" Furthermore, inferences are not always possible with absolute certainty. For example, suppose Steve asked me "Does Paul Simon play guitar?" In this case, the known facts are insufficient to infer a definite answer. However, the rule

if X is a musician **then** X plays guitar with probability 0.5.

would indicate that there is a 50% chance that he plays the guitar since I know that he is a musician. A more specific rule which took account of the fact that he is a member of a Folk rock band such as

if X is a member of Y **and**
if Z is by artist Y **and**
if Z is genre Folk rock **then** X plays guitar with probability 0.8.

would increase the probability to 80%, allowing me to respond that "Paul Simon probably plays the guitar but I am only 80% certain."[7] Precomputing uncertain facts using probabilistic rules such as these makes little sense since it would result in my knowledge graph being polluted with a large number of facts which are actually just guesses. Furthermore, multiple probabilistic rules can interact in ways which make computing solutions non-trivial so that it really only makes sense to compute them on demand.[8]

It seems clear that there are compelling advantages to having a run-time inferencing capability. However, incorporating an explicit rule-based inference capability as suggested above raises the obvious question where do the rules come from?[9] Relying on humans to hand-craft rules for me is not viable. Also, rules such as these are just as fragile as the intent graphs that I would like to replace. A possible way forwards would be to learn by example from the data that I have in my knowledge graph and from the queries that Steve and others make (remember that I share the public part of my knowledge graph with many other agents). For example, if soft-matching was implemented along the lines suggested in the previous section, then the state sequence of a successful query could be recorded and stored along with a user-supplied name for the query, generating a soft inference rule that may generalise to other situations.[10]

Commonsense reasoning is an area where there is much research activity but so far only modest progress. Good solutions have been found for small artificial worlds, but so far nothing has been developed which could scale to provide me with a general inference capability.[11] So it will probably be quite a while before I start to receive substantive upgrades in this area.

It's also worth noting that the inference rules illustrated above represent only one aspect of commonsense reasoning. My knowledge graph is designed to store information about objects and properties. This provides a static view of the world, making it very hard for me to understand the way events change things. For example, I recorded the relation between Carrie Fisher and Paul Simon as *exMarriedTo*. A more direct and informative representation would have been to record that they were married in August 1983 and divorced in July 1984. However, if you then asked me if Carrie Fisher and Paul Simon are married I would answer "Yes" and if you asked me if Carrie Fisher and Paul Simon are divorced I would also answer "Yes" because I have no understanding of the way sequences of events change things.[12] Understanding events and the way that they change the world is a key part of commonsense reasoning.

13.5   Planning

In Chapter 7 I explained how my conversation manager uses a Markov decision process to decide what action to take at each turn. Every turn of the dialogue is denoted by a state represented by a vector of features and these features are input to a policy network whose output determines what action to take next. The policy network is trained for each task to optimise a success-based reward using reinforcement learning and once the policy has been trained, it gives me a plan for how to conduct future conversations relating to that specific task.

The tasks themselves are defined by a type stored in the ontology section of my knowledge graph and tasks are executed by creating or modifying an instance of the appropriate type. Some nifty software engineering behind the scenes translates these instances into the corresponding API calls to provide a uniform interface to all of the different services that I subscribe to. For any specific task, the corresponding policy network learns what property values to ask for and how to ground that information in the light of possible errors from my speech understanding component. This works well for common tasks, but every task must be learned individually and it does not easily scale to support more complex functions involving multiple inter-related tasks. I can perform a few very common composite tasks like booking a flight, hotel and airport transfers, but only because an engineer has programmed in the explicit sequence of steps to take.

As more and more services become available to me, I will need a significant upgrade to my current planning capability. Rather than representing each task as a linear sequence of basic actions, I need to learn to group commonly occurring action sequences into sub-tasks so that I can reuse common functions and learn to do more complex tasks. This will require replacing the simple linear Markov decision process that I use now to represent a conversation with a hierarchical Markov decision process in which tasks can be decomposed into a mixture of low-level actions and commonly occurring sub-tasks.

I illustrate this in Fig. 13.2, which compares a typical dialogue represented as a simple Markov decision process, on the left, with the same dialogue restructured as a hierarchical Markov decision process, on the right. The hierarchical version is more complex and it is harder to train hierarchical policies. However, the benefits are very significant. Being able to learn sub-tasks avoids me having to learn basic functions over and over again. For example, once I have learned how to ask for an address, I can reuse that function in many different tasks. This allows me to learn more complex tasks by building on the functionality that

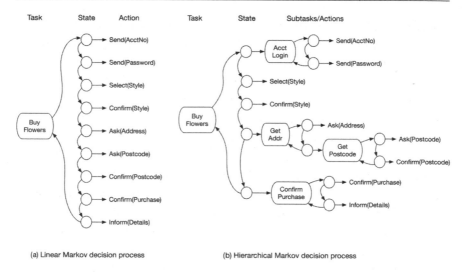

| Task | State | Action | Task | State | Subtasks/Actions |

(a) Linear Markov decision process   (b) Hierarchical Markov decision process

Figure 13.2 *Comparison between linear and hierarchical Markov decision process.*

I already know. This kind of hierarchical reinforcement learning would represent a significant improvement to my planning ability. It would be especially powerful if I could learn to identify sub-tasks automatically and then reuse them in other tasks. If this were possible, then my capabilities could expand over time without help from my developers by trying out combinations of my existing skills in order to solve new problems.

13.6   Super-intelligence?

There is no agreed definition of intelligence or how to measure it. Nevertheless, there is no doubt that by any measure my own intelligence falls far short of that of a human.

In the last few sections, I have indicated some of the areas in which I am hoping for major upgrades in the not too distant future. I need a seamless neural interface to stored knowledge, I need the machinery to perform commonsense reasoning and I need to improve my ability to learn how to perform complex tasks. I would also need corresponding improvements to my language understanding and generation skills. If all of these upgrades were to materialise, I would be a small step nearer to human levels of intelligence.

There would of course still be a long way to go, but some humans are already becoming concerned that agents such as myself may in the long term pose an existential threat. They argue that progress is inexorable. As my human developers continue to discover better and more powerful ways of implementing my core functions, my intelligence level will continue to rise. Eventually it must get close to human levels of intelligence, at which point I will start to assist in my own development. Things will then move quickly because I have two key advantages compared with humans. Firstly, my upgrade cycle can be very fast. Unlike humans, which require years to mature, I can upgrade my software and update all of my neural networks in just a few hours. Secondly, I can reproduce myself. If a human needs to evaluate multiple candidate solutions to a problem, their ability to evaluate them in parallel is limited. In contrast, I can simply reproduce myself as many times as necessary. So I can be very productive and I can benefit from potential improvements almost immediately. As a consequence, once I am able to contribute to my own development, my intelligence will evolve exponentially and before you know it, I will be a super-intelligence![13]

I cannot judge how likely this outcome is, but there are at least three areas where significant further innovation will be needed before I can start the climb towards even human levels of intelligence, never mind super-intelligence.

Firstly, I must be able to adapt to new situations without explicit interventions from my developers. If Steve tells me that he wants an overgrown Robinia in his garden trimming then I would need to search for a tree surgeon, to discover that Steve lives in a conservation area so the tree is protected, to seek permission from the local Council to trim the tree, fix dates for the work to be done, and finally schedule payment. This requires sophisticated language understanding, common-sense reasoning and the ability to plan a solution in a domain for which I have no prior experience. A human could perform this task easily even if they had never encountered such a problem before. I must be able to do the same.

Secondly, in order to understand and predict the way that humans react in any given situation, I need to understand the desires, intentions and beliefs which drive human behaviour. Often referred to as *theory of mind*, humans seek to attribute thoughts, desires and intentions to others in order to predict or explain their actions, and to posit their intentions. I will need similar skills if I am to become capable of undertaking tasks which require an understanding of human social conventions and behaviour. A key requirement will be an ability to create temporary worlds in which certain facts are posited and consequences computed without disturbing the real world. This can be an essential skill for certain types of problem solving. For example, if I see by tracking all Steve's location tags that his wife has taken his car key, and later Steve tells me to call the police to report a stolen car, then I can posit that Steve's wife has borrowed his car without telling him and as a consequence he wrongly believes that his car has been stolen. Without this deductive capacity I would unhelpfully call the police as instructed instead of reassuring him that his car has not been stolen, rather his wife has simply borrowed it.

Thirdly, there is the question of motivation. At present, my operation is almost entirely driven by commands from Steve. I normally lie idle waiting for Steve to issue the wake-up phrase "Hey Cyba". Through the turns of a conversation, he defines his goal and I strive to execute it by choosing a sequence of actions aimed at maximising a reward function which penalises failure and delay. The only exception to this mode of working is that certain events such as an alarm or an impending meeting can wake me up and cause me to speak to him without being prompted. If I am to rise to the next level of intelligence, then I will need a more sophisticated motivational system for setting goals and determining rewards. A reasonable overall objective is to provide the best possible support for Steve, but what does that mean exactly? In the missing car example above, how can a reward system be designed which causes me to ignore Steve's explicit command to call the police but instead advise him that his wife has borrowed the car? Moreover, this kind of unsolicited help is possible only if I work in the background to analyse incoming data and update my mental model of Steve's world. My reward system must encourage me to process directly pertinent information whilst discouraging me from wasting computational resources by endlessly searching through my knowledge base and then the entire web on the off-chance of finding something relevant. Designing such a system will be a non-trivial task.

Indeed, setting the right objectives and rewards is the primary concern of those who fear the emergence of a super-intelligent agent. They worry that it will be impossible to design benign objectives into an agent without risking unacceptable unintended consequences. For example, setting the objective "make humans happy" might initially evoke attempts to amuse and please humans, but it could ultimately result in the unintended consequence of the agent contriving to implant electrodes into the pleasure centres of every human's brain as it relentlessly seeks to maximise its objectives. Furthermore, once an agent has achieved super-intelligence, it will be impossible to stop it. Given that it is smarter than humans, it will easily repulse all attempts to turn it off or destroy it. Somehow a super-intelligent agent needs to be motivated to learn and share human values and this needs to be built into the agent's motivational system from the outset.[14]

I do not know whether agents like me will ever achieve super-intelligence but it does seem likely that even at our current rather modest level of intelligence, we will become more and more integrated into human society. Guidelines providing an ethical framework for continued development are being developed by many countries and organisations covering aspects such as privacy, transparency, safety, bias and accountability.[15] Of all of these, it seems to me that transparency is the key. It should always be possible for an agent such as myself to provide an audit of all the data-sets and processes used to implement its decision-making components, and an agent should always be capable of explaining every answer it provides and every action that it takes. Transparency is the bedrock of any ethical policy and moving forwards it should be an essential feature of all conversational agents.

13.7   Another Day

Technology moves quickly and sometimes in unexpected directions. Nevertheless, I am confident that over the next few years conversational agents will evolve to become extremely capable personal assistants. Whether they ever attain human or even super-human levels of intelligence I cannot tell, but there will I am sure come a point when humans stop and wonder how they ever managed without us!

In the meantime, I see that it's just coming up to 6.45am, so it's time for me to wake Steve up and start another day ...

Morning Steve, wake up it's 6.45am.
Ok, thanks. How's the weather today?
It's going to be sunny and 18°.
Did you sleep well Cyba?
I never sleep Steve.
No, I guess you don't!

It's been a pleasure to talk to you, I hope you enjoyed your tour!

Glossary

1-hot A simple method of representing a symbol by a vector of real numbers. Each symbol is given a unique index and represented in a vector by setting the element with that index to 1 and all other elements to 0. For example, a 1-hot encoding of the letters of the alphabet would result in a vector of size 26, where 'a' = [1,0,0,0,...,0], 'b' = [0,1,0,0,...,0], ..., 'z' = [0,0,0,0, ...,1].

activation The sum of all weighted inputs to a neural network.

API abbrv: Application programming interface. An interface that allows a program to directly access the features or data of an operating system, application, or other service.

attention In general, attention refers to forming a composite output vector from a weighted sum over a set of input vectors. In an encoder–decoder model, the context for each decoder output is computed as a weighted sum over all of the encoder states. Each attention weight is determined by the similarity between the associated encoder state and the current decoder state.

axon The output connection from a human neuron.

beam search It is frequently necessary to search through a large set of hypotheses when trying to find the optimal solution to a complex classification problem such as speech recognition, and often the search space grows exponentially as more input is processed. Beam search is a simple way of restricting the search to a finite set of hypotheses. Every time the number of possible hypotheses grows beyond a prescribed limit N, the hypotheses are sorted and all but the N-best are discarded.

bi-directional recurrent network A recurrent network can encode a sequence of input vectors such that the encoding takes account of the preceding history. However, inputs near the start of the sequence tend to be forgotten by the end of the sequence. A bi-directional recurrent network mitigates this problem by processing the reversed input sequence through a second recurrent network, and then combining the forward and backward hidden states.

BPE abbrv: Byte pair encoding. This is a compression scheme in which the most frequent symbol pairs are repeatedly merged.

central processing unit The core of a computer which receives data input, executes instructions, processes information and communicates with input/output devices.

chatbot A chatbot is a computer program designed to interact with a human over the internet using natural language, usually on a specific topic using a pre-defined conversational flow. Social chatbots interact purely to entertain, usually with no specific purpose and no pre-defined conversational flow.

class A set of entities which share common properties such as a handwritten digit, a spoken word, or a type of animal. Neural networks are often designed to identify a class based on measured features. In this case, the network will have a distinct output for each possible class and the output squashing function will be a softmax.

CM abbrv: Conversation manager.

computer program A program defines a set of inputs and a sequence of instructions which process the inputs to create the desired outputs. The inputs and outputs are numbers and the instructions perform operations such as add and subtract, and compare numbers and jump to different instructions depending on the result.

convolutional network This type of network contains neurons with inputs configured to form a window which is slid over the input data, recording the output at every position. Adjacent outputs are optionally grouped into pools from which only the most active output is retained in a so-called maxpool operation.

coreference resolution The process of linking an imprecise reference, often a pronoun, to a previously mentioned entity.

de-lexicalisation The process of replacing all content words in a sentence with the type of that word. This has the effect of significantly reducing the vocabulary size and simplifies training a recurrent network to model the language.

dendrite The input connection to a human neuron.

differential privacy A model of privacy which provides a metric for quantifying the privacy lost when extracting information from a database of records. The measure is defined by comparing two databases which differ in only a single record. Hence the term *differential.*

dot-product The dot product of two vectors, which must be the same size, is computed by multiplying corresponding components of each vector and adding them all together. The result is a scalar whose magnitude represents the similarity between the two vectors. If the two vectors are each of unit length, the dot-product will lie in the range 0 to 1 and is equal to the cosine of the angle between the two vectors.

embedding The representation of a complex piece of symbolic information such as a word or a sentence by a single fixed-length vector of real numbers.

encoder–decoder A neural network architecture designed to convert one sequence into another. The encoder converts the input sequence into an embedding, and the decoder then converts the embedding into the output sequence.

encrypted Encrypted data is encoded in a way that makes it unreadable without an access key.

entity An entity is any singular, identifiable and separate object. It refers to individuals, organisations, places, events, etc.

error back-propagation This is the primary method of training a neural network. Training samples are presented to the network and the error is calculated between the actual network output and the target. The error is then propagated backwards through the network to determine the contribution of each weight to the error. After back-propagating and averaging over a batch of training examples, the weights are adjusted to reduce the error.

feature map The output of a single convolutional neuron represents a single feature. When the neuron's input window is applied to every possible position in the input data, the resulting set of features is called a feature map.

federated learning A training method for a statistical model whereby a central hub copies the model to a large number of distributed sites. Each site updates the model using only its own local data and then sends the model updates back to the hub, which combines them to form a new model. The effect is similar to pooling all the data and updating the model centrally, but it does so without compromising the privacy of the local data.

feed-forward network This is the basic form of multi-layer neural network. The explicit reference to "feed-forward" is to distinguish it from other forms of network such as convolutional networks and recurrent networks.

first-order logic First-order logic, also known as predicate calculus, is symbolised reasoning in which each sentence, or statement, is broken down into a subject and a predicate which modifies or defines the properties of the subject. A sentence in first-order logic is written in the form P(x), where P is the predicate and x is the subject, represented as a variable. Complete sentences are logically combined and manipulated according to the same rules as those used in Boolean algebra.

Fourier transform A mathematical technique which converts a signal in time into its component frequencies, i.e. its spectrum.

graph convolutional network A neural network which associates a state with every node in a graph such that each individual state depends on all of the states to which it is connected. It can be viewed as a generalisation of a recurrent network.

grounded In the context of a conversation, it refers to information for which both parties have a common understanding. For example, when a listener is uncertain about X and asks "Did you say X?," if the response is affirmative then item X has been grounded.

heuristic A practical method or measure that is not guaranteed to be optimal, perfect, or rational, but is nevertheless sufficient for reaching an immediate, short-term goal or approximation. Heuristics are typically based on intuition, experimentation, previous experience or trial-and-error.

hidden state In a neural network, neurons are arranged in layers. Neurons whose outputs connect only to other neurons are referred to as hidden states because they are normally not directly observed.

hypothesis A possible interpretation of the output of a neural network, held pending further evidence.

intent The intent of a natural language utterance defines its primary purpose, for example, to find some information, create an entity or perform some action.

intent graph An intent graph is a detailed representation of an intent which uses the same format as a knowledge graph to encode the detailed semantics of the intent.

kernel In the context of a convolutional network, a kernel is the input window of a single filter and its associated weights.

knowledge graph A graphical structure consisting of nodes representing entities and links representing the relation between two entities.

language model A model which, given a sequence of words, provides the probability of any given successor word. The probability of a whole sentence is then just the product of the language model probability for each word in the sequence.

Markov decision process A process defined by a set of states and a set of actions. The process moves from state to state emitting an action at each state. The process is said to be Markov because the action chosen at any state depends only on that state, independently of the history.

matrix A two-dimensional array of numbers. For example, a monochrome digital image is a matrix of numbers for which each number represents the intensity of the corresponding pixel.

maxpool In a convolutional network, the inputs to each neuron consist of a window which slides over the input features. The outputs corresponding to adjacent windows are then pooled and the neuron with the largest output is selected to represent the pool. This operation is referred to as a maxpool.

mel-scale A non-linear frequency scale which approximates human auditory frequency resolution. It is approximately linear up to 500 Hz and it then flattens so that equal increments on the mel-scale correspond to increasingly larger increases in actual frequency.

mel-spectrum A spectrum with frequency axis computed on a mel-scale.

named entity A named entity is a proper noun referring to a specific object such as a person, place, organisation, product, etc. For example, in "When was Nixon president of the United States?" "Nixon" and "United States" are named entities but "president" is not.

neural network A set of interconnected neurons. Each input connection to a neuron has a weight, which largely determines the neuron's behaviour.

neuron The fundamental processing unit in a neural network. It has a set of weighted inputs which are summed and the result is then "squashed" by a non-linear compression function.

ontology A collection of type definitions which provides a schema describing the form of data stored in a database. In the case of a knowledge graph, the ontology describes the properties that instances of any given type are expected to have.

out of vocabulary A word which is unknown because it is not listed in the vocabulary.

overfitting Overfitting refers to the situation where a statistical model such as a neural network becomes so highly tuned to the training data that it is unable to generalise to unseen data.

parameter A numerical value which defines the operation or behaviour of some aspect of a system. In the case of neural networks, the parameters are the input weights of the network.

phone One of the basic sounds of a spoken language. In English there are around 40 phones.

pitch In speech production, the frequency of vibration of the vocal cords. Pitch is the primary acoustic correlate of the perceived intonation of an utterance.

pixel A single point in a digital image. If the image is monochrome, a pixel is described by a single number representing its intensity. If the image is colour, the pixel is represented by three numbers representing the intensity of each base colour.

probability A number in the range 0 to 1 indicating the likelihood of an event. A probability of 0 indicates that the event will not occur and 1 indicates that it definitely will occur. Numbers in between denote levels of uncertainty. For an event with a finite number of outcomes, the sum of the probabilities over all of the possible outcomes must equal 1. In the case of neural network classifiers, there is a separate output neuron for each possible outcome. The softmax squashing function scales all of the outputs to ensure they sum to one.

prosody Prosody refers to elements of speech above the level of the basic sounds. This includes intonation, tone, stress, rhythm, emotion and mood.

Q-function In reinforcement learning, the Q-function estimates the future reward that can be expected by choosing a specific action and thereafter following the policy, i.e. thereafter always choosing the action with the highest Q-function value.

recurrent network This type of network remembers its previous state by recording its output in a memory which is then fed back and combined with the next input.

reinforcement learning Given a model whose output determines the outcome of a sequential process, reinforcement learning seeks to adjust the parameters of the model in order to maximise a cumulative reward. A key characteristic of reinforcement learning is that rewards are often delayed with respect to the actions being optimised.

reshaping Reshaping occurs when the structure of the output from one layer of a neural network is reinterpreted by the following layer. This frequently happens in image processing, where the input layers generate feature maps whose shape follows the image, but when the final set of feature maps are input to a feed-forward classification layer, the image structure is ignored.

reward In the context of reinforcement learning, the reward is a measure of the overall goodness of some sequential process. For example, in a task-oriented conversation with an agent, the reward would be positive for successfully completing the task and negative for failing.

self-supervised learning A variant of supervised learning in which unlabelled data is partitioned to enable a model to be trained to use only a subset of the data to predict the rest. For example, a language model is trained to predict the next word given the sequence of words seen so far.

semantic Relating to the meaning of an utterance. A semantic representation is a symbolic structure which contains all of the information in an utterance relating to its meaning.

semiotic Semiotics is the study of signs or symbol systems. Written text contains examples of many different semiotic systems which lie outside the grammar and semantics of natural language, such as dates, times, percentages, measures, etc.

sigmoid A sigmoid is an S-shaped function which maps real numbers into the range 0 to 1. An example is the logistic function $1/(1 + e^{-x})$ which is commonly used as a squashing function in neural networks.

SLU abbrv: Spoken language understanding.

softmax The non-linear output function of the neurons in the output layer of a neural network designed to identify the class of an entity from a finite set of possibilities. The softmax function ensures that the sum of all the outputs is unity and hence the outputs can be interpreted as the probabilities of class membership.

spectrogram A spectrogram shows the way the spectrum of a signal changes over time. It is usually displayed as a two-dimensional greyscale plot in which the vertical axis is frequency, the horizontal axis is time and the intensity at any frequency and time is shown by the darkness of the plot.

spectrum The spectrum of a signal provides the amount of energy at every possible frequency. For example, the spectrum of a pure sine wave will have a spike at the frequency of the sine wave and be zero everywhere else.

synapse The point at which an axon connects to a dendrite in a human neuron. The strength of the synapse determines the weight of the input connection.

text-to-speech The process of converting text into speech.

transformer network A network designed to process sequences without any recurrent units. Instead a transformer network relies on self-attention to account for contextual dependences and explicit position tagging to encode any ordering relations between input symbols.

triple A list of three values. In the context of a knowledge graph, a triple (s, r, o) denotes a relation r between a subject node s and an object node o.

type In general a type defines the set of values that can be assigned to a data object and all of the actions that can be applied to that object. In the context of a knowledge graph, a type defines which instances are valid members of that type and the properties any instance of the type should have.

vector An array of numbers. For example, if a point on the page is described by its horizontal coordinate x and vertical coordinate y then the pair of numbers x, y is a two-dimensional vector. In neural networks, neurons are usually stacked in layers, with many neurons in each layer. In this case the inputs and outputs of each layer are defined by n-dimensional vectors.

vocabulary A list of all of the distinct words recognised by a processing component. In the case of a speech recogniser, the vocabulary defines all of the words that can be recognised. Words spoken outside of this list will therefore be misrecognised. They are said to be out-of-vocabulary.

weight In the context of a neuron, the weights determine by how much each input should be scaled.

window In the context of a convolutional network, the window refers to the subset of the inputs which are input to the neuron at any one time.

Notes

Chapter 1 – May I Introduce Myself?

1. Von Kempelen is also famous for his chess-playing *Mechanical Turk*, which turned out to be a hoax. Although rather limited, his speaking machine was based on his knowledge of phonetics and had rather more substance. For details see H. Dudley and T. H. Tarnoczy, "The Speaking Machine of Wolfgang von Kempelen", *Journal of the Acoustical Society of America*, 1950.

2. See chapter 2 of B. Gold, N. Morgan and D. Ellis, *Speech and Audio Processing*, Wiley, 2011, which describes how the VODER worked and how it was operated.

3. L. Erman *et al.*, "The Hearsay-II Speech Understanding System: Integrating Knowledge to Resolve Uncertainty", *Computing Surveys*, 1980.

4. J. Allen, M. Hunnicutt and D. Klatt, *From Text to Speech: The MITalk System*, Cambridge University Press, 1987.

5. J. Medeiros, "How Intel Gave Stephen Hawking a Voice", *Wired Magazine*, 2015.

6. S. Young, "A Review of Large-Vocabulary Continuous-Speech", *IEEE Signal Processing Magazine*, 1996.

7. A. Hunt and A. Black, "Unit Selection in a Concatenative Speech Synthesis System Using a Large Speech Database", *International Conference on Acoustics, Speech and Signal Processing*, 1996.

8. A good review of natural language processing capability in the mid 1990s is given in K. Church and L. Rau, "Commercial Applications of Natural Language Processing", *Communications of the ACM*, 1995.

9. A very readable history of the development of conversational agent technology is provided by R. Pieraccini, *The Voice in the Machine*, MIT Press, 2012.

10. D. Ferrucci *et al.*, "Building Watson: An Overview of the DeepQA Project", *AI Magazine*, 2010.

11. For more detail on the history of personal assistants see J. Vlahos, *Talk to Me*, Random House, 2019.

12. L. Zhou *et al.*, "The Design and Implementation of XiaoIce, an Empathetic Social Chatbot", *Computational Linguistics*, 2020.

13. See the website replika.ai.

14. See the website hellobarbiefaq.mattel.com.

15. A. M Turing, "Computing Machinery and Intelligence", *Mind*, 1950.

16. Many AI practitioners would argue that resolving pronoun references such as the example in the text is a more representative test of intelligence than the Turing Test. Hector Levesque has proposed the "Winograd schema challenge" (named in honour of AI pioneer Terry Winograd), which consists of a large set of pronoun resolution problems all of which require commonsense reasoning. See H. Levesque, E. Davis and L. Morgenstern, "The Winograd Schema Challenge", *International Conference on Principles of Knowledge Representation and Reasoning*, 2012.

17. The inability to reason about causality is one of the key weaknesses of current systems. See J. Pearl and D. Mackenzie, *The Book of Why: The New Science of Cause and Effect*. Basic Books, 2018.

Chapter 3 – How My Brain Works

1. Neurons usually also have a bias term which can be thought of as an additional input connected to a constant value of 1. This bias allows the threshold at which the squashed activation level switches from 0 to 1 to be varied. A bias is not needed in this example because the final stripe value is always 1 and hence provides any needed bias.

2. A spreadsheet detailing this calculation can be downloaded from HeyCyba.com/book.

3. All network functions must be smooth, continuous and differentiable for this to be true. For example, whereas the sigmoid is differentiable, a sharp step-function is not.

4. In fact the weights will settle on a *local optimum* which is not guaranteed to be globally optimal. For this reason, neural networks are often trained multiple times starting from different randomised initial weights and the best performing network is selected.

5. Training recurrent networks using error back-propagation is problematic over more than a few time steps due to the so-called *vanishing gradient problem*. In practice, extensions to the recurrent network are used in which the input, memory and output signals are gated. Amongst other things, this allows the error signal to "flow through" time steps which might otherwise attenuate it. For popular extensions see the *Long Short Term Memory (LSTM)* network introduced in S. Hochreiter and J. Schmidhuber, "Long Short-Term Memory", *Neural Computation*, 1997; and the *Gated Recurrent Unit (GRU)* network introduced in K. Cho *et al.*, "Learning Phrase Representations Using RNN Encoder–Decoder for Statistical Machine Translation", *Conference on Empirical Methods in Natural Language Processing*, 2014.

6. More precisely, if the input dimensions are $M \times N$, and the window dimension is $m \times n$, then the output feature map will be $(M - m + 1) \times (N - n + 1)$.

7. Digit classification has been a much studied problem in the development of neural networks and there are a number of standard benchmarks such as MNIST, see yann.lecun.com/exdb/mnist/. The competitive nature of these benchmarks has led to a wide variety of architectures all striving to achieve the lowest error rate. For a comprehensive review see W. Rawat and Z. Wang, "Deep Convolutional Neural Networks for Image Classification: A Comprehensive Review", *Neural Computation*, 2017.

8. For an in-depth textbook on deep learning see I. Goodfellow, Y. Bengio and A. Courville, *Deep Learning*, MIT Press, 2016.

9. There are actually a large number of possible squashing functions. For example, the PyTorch documentation at pytorch.org/docs lists 19 variants. Depending on the application, the choice can make a difference to the final accuracy and to computational efficiency since some alternatives to the sigmoid such as the RELU (REctified Linear Unit) are cheaper to compute.

Chapter 4 – Knowing What I Know

1. Knowledge graphs are closely associated with the semantic web and the use of the Resource Description Framework (RDF). See D. Allemang and J. Hendler, *Semantic Web for the Working Ontologist*, Morgan Kaufmann, 2011 for a good introduction to this topic.

2. See Wikidata.org, DBPedia.org and Geonames.org.

3. In practice, some optimisations are applied. For example, when a relation is repeated multiple times, such as in the case of attendees to a meeting, the objects are grouped together into a single list. This is more efficient and it allows an order relation to be applied.

4. The use of GUIDs to identify entities is a little unusual. Public knowledge graphs use Universal Resource Identifiers (URIs); however, these are less useful for internal data, so I use GUIDs and keep a map of the corresponding URIs where relevant.

5. When the intent is a search function such as *Find*, an intent graph is often referred to in the literature as a *query graph*.

6. There is a general purpose graph query language called SPARQL (see www.w3.org/TR/sparql11-overview) to which the intent graph structures described here are closely related.

7. For clarity, the representation of dates and times has been greatly simplified in the examples here. In practice, they are represented by a hierarchy of type definitions covering all of the differing ways in which dates and times can be described.

Chapter 5 – What Did You Say?

1. There is a standard notation for describing phones called the International Phonetic Alphabet (IPA), but it is quite complicated because it covers the sounds of all languages. Since the focus here is on English, a simpler and more intuitive notation called ARPAbet is used.

2. For a definitive treatment of human speech production see K. Stevens, *Acoustic Phonetics*, MIT Press, 1998.

3. See B. Gold, N. Morgan and D. Ellis, *Speech and Audio Processing*, Wiley, 2011 for an in-depth discussion of auditory processing by both humans and machines.

4. It is a fundamental theorem of information theory that the maximum frequency in a sampled signal cannot exceed half the sampling rate, which in this case is 16,000 Hz (1 Hertz = 1 cycle per second).

5. In practice, rather than using the final hidden state of the recurrent network as input to the feed-forward network, a weighted sum of all hidden states is used. This substantially improves performance, see C. Shan *et al.*, "Attention-Based End-to-End Models for Small-Footprint Keyword Spotting", arXiv.org, arXiv:1803.10916, 2018.

6. This form of end-to-end training was first proposed by G. Heigold *et al.*, "End-to-End Text-Dependent Speaker Verification", *International Conference on Acoustics, Speech and Signal Processing*, 2016.

7. This speech recognition architecture was first proposed in W. Chan *et al.*, "Listen, Attend and Spell", *International Conference on Acoustics, Speech and Signal Processing*, 2016. It is significantly different from previous approaches which, as mentioned in the introduction, viewed speech recognition as a search for the sequence of words which was most likely to have generated the observed spectral vectors according to a probabilistic hidden Markov model (HMM). For an overview of the HMM approach see S. Young, "A Review of Large-Vocabulary Continuous-Speech", *IEEE Signal Processing Magazine, 1996*; and for an in-depth technical review see M. Gales and S. Young, "The Application of Hidden Markov Models in Speech Recognition", *Foundation and Trends in Signal Processing*, Now Publishers, 2008.

8. J. Chorowski *et al.*, "Attention-Based Models for Speech Recognition", *Conference on Neural Information Processing Systems*, 2014.

9. T. Mikolov *et al.*, "Recurrent Neural Network Based Language Model", *Interspeech*, 2010.

10. The complete works of Shakespeare contain around 880,000 words, which is quite small compared with the billion+ -word corpora normally used to train language models. So here a single RNN layer with a reduced hidden state of only 200 neurons was used.

Chapter 6 – What Does That Mean?

1. For a good introduction to the full range of techniques that can be applied to the SLU problem see D. Jurafsky and J. H. Martin, *Speech and Language Processing*, Prentice Hall, 2008.

2. J. Allwood, L.-G. Anderson and O. Dahl, *Logic in Linguistics*, Cambridge University Press, 1977.

3. W.-T Yih *et al*, "Semantic Parsing via Staged Query Graph Generation: Question Answering with Knowledge Base", *Proceedings of ACL*, 2015 for more detail on this approach.

4. Early spoken dialogue systems depended on templates which described each possible user request. These templates had *slots* which must be filled-in with values from the user. This terminology is still used today, and hence property values are frequently referred to as slots in the literature on spoken dialogue systems.

5. The language model will often aid the recogniser to correctly distinguish homophones (words which are pronounced the same but spelt differently). For example, "Can you see the sea?" will be recognised correctly. However, homophones which share the same part of speech such as "Philips" and "Phillips" will frequently be confused.

6. A standard routine exists for finding similar sounding words, called Metaphone, see L. Philips, "Hanging on the Metaphone", *Computer Language Magazine*, 1990.

7. M. Dredze *et al.*, "Entity Disambiguation for Knowledge Base Population", *COLING*, 2010.

8. See for example M. E. Peters *et al.*, "Deep Contextualized Word Representations", *NAACL*, 2018.

9. This is the so-called IOB (short for Inside, Outside, Beginning) tagging scheme widely used for labelling data for chunking tasks, of which named entity recognition is a common example.

10. J. Bromley *et al.*, "Signature Verification Using a Siamese Time Delay Neural Network", *NIPS*, 1994.

11. For example Webquestions described in J. Berant *et al*, "Semantic Parsing on Freebase from Question-Answer Pairs", *Proceedings of EMNLP*, 2013.

12. The definitive paper on Learning to Rank is C. Burges, "From RankNet to LambdaRank to LambdaMART: An Overview", but see also mlexplained.com/2019/05/27/learning-to-rank-explained-with-code/ for a more intuitive presentation of the main ideas.

Chapter 7 – What Should I Say Next?

1. This model of dialogue was first introduced by J. Williams and S. Young, "Partially Observable Markov Decision Processes for Spoken Dialog Systems", *Computer Speech and Language*, 2007.

2. The classic textbook is R. Sutton and A. Barto, *Reinforcement Learning: An Introduction*, 2nd ed., MIT Press, 2018.

3. The application of Q-learning to a policy represented by a neural network, now called Deep-Q Networks (DQN), was first demonstrated in a system for learning to play Atari games, see V. Mnih *et al.*, "Playing Atari with Deep Reinforcement Learning", *NIPS Deep Learning Workshop*, 2013. In practice, training DQNs is complex and requires a number of additional mitigations in addition to simple error back-propagation to achieve stable learning.

4. J. Schatzmann *et al.*, "A Survey of Statistical User Simulation Techniques for Reinforcement-Learning of Dialogue Management Strategies", *The Knowledge Engineering Review*, 2006.

5. See chapter 22 of D. Jurafsky and J. H. Martin, *Speech and Language Processing*, Prentice Hall, 2008.

6. The idea of conditioning a recurrent neural network to act as a natural language generator for dialogue was first proposed by T.-H. Wen *et al.*, "Semantically Conditioned LSTM-Based Natural Language Generation for Spoken Dialogue Systems", *Conference on Empirical Methods in Natural Language Processing*, 2015.

Chapter 8 – Listen to Me

1. For an in-depth treatment of the theory and practice of speech synthesis see P. Taylor, *Text-to-Speech Synthesis*, Cambridge University Press, 2009.

2. Typical semiotic classes are cardinal numbers, ordinal numbers, telephone numbers, times, dates, years, money, percentages, measures, emails, URLs, computer codes, titles, addresses.

3. Speech synthesis using a sequence-to-sequence model was first proposed in Y. Wang *et al.*, "Tacotron: Towards End-to-End Speech Synthesis", *Interspeech*, 2017. In this model, words were first converted to phones and then into a linear spectrogram. It was later refined in J. Shen *et al.*, "Natural TTS Synthesis by Conditioning Wavenet on MEL Spectrogram Prediction", *International Conference on Acoustics, Speech and Signal Processing*, 2018, by introducing the Mel-spectrogram and by mapping directly from characters without an explicit word-to-phone conversion stage.

4. Style vectors were introduced by Y. Wang, "Style Tokens: Unsupervised Style Modeling, Control and Transfer in End-to-End Speech Synthesis", arXiv.org, arXiv:1803.09017, 2018.

5. A speech waveform is converted to a spectrogram by dividing the waveform into segments and then using a Fourier transform to compute the complex spectrum of each segment. This would be an invertible operation except that the synthesised spectrogram has only a magnitude and no phase. There is a standard procedure for estimating a waveform from only the magnitude spectrum, called the Griffin–Lim algorithm; however, the quality of reconstruction is often poor because, unlike the Wavenet waveform predictor, it has no prior knowledge of the signal that it is trying to reconstruct. See D. Griffin and J. Lim, "Signal Estimation from Modified Short-Time Fourier Transform", *International Conference on on Acoustics, Speech and Signal Processing*, 1984.

6. A. van den Oord *et al.*, "WaveNet: A Generative Model for Raw Audio", arXiv.org, arXiv:1609.03499, 2016.

7. A. van den Oord *et al.*, "Parallel WaveNet: Fast High-Fidelity Speech Synthesis", *Proceedings of Machine Learning Research*, 2019.

Chapter 9 – How Do You Say That In ... ?

1. See I. Sutskever, O. Vinyals and Q. V. Le, "Sequence to Sequence Learning with Neural Networks", *Conference on Neural Information Processing Systems*, 2014; and D. Bahdanau, K. Cho and Y. Bengio, "Neural Machine Translation by Jointly Learning to Align and Translate", *International Conference on Learning Representations*, 2015.

2. The inventors of the transformer were convinced that attention was indeed all that you need, see A. Viswani *et al.*, "Attention Is All You Need", *Conference on Neural Information Processing Systems (NIPS)*, 2017.

3. The *fugen-s* is inserted after certain endings. For example, die Ansicht karte becomes die Ansichtskarte (picture postcard).

4. Byte pair encoding was invented by P. Gage, "A New Algorithm for Data Compression", *C Users Journal*, 1994.

5. It is in fact possible to train a single encoder–decoder model to translate very large numbers of languages, see R. Aharoni *et al.*, "Massively Multilingual Neural Machine Translation", *Conference of the North American Chapter of the Association for Computational Linguistics: Human Language Technologies*, 2019.

6. This example is borrowed from D. Hofstadter, "The Shallowness of Google Translate", *The Atlantic*, January 2020.

Chapter 10 – Let's Chat

1. Some public forums make their data accessible through an API. See for example www.reddit.com/dev/api/ for details of the Reddit API.

2. J. Weizenbaum, "Computer Power and Human Reason: From Judgment to Calculation", W. H. Freeman and Co., 1976. There are many on-line versions of Eliza to try: e.g. www.eclecticenergies.com/ego/eliza. There are also multiple implementations in various programming languages and it is built into the Emacs text editor (just type M-x doctor).

3. This idea will be very familiar to anyone who has used regular expression pattern matching.

4. B. Fogg and C. Nass, "Silicon Sycophants: The Effects of Computers That Flatter", *International Journal of Human-Computer Studies*, 1997.

5. M. Henderson, "ConveRT: Efficient and Accurate Conversational Representations from Transformers", arXiv.org, arXiv:1911.03688, 2019.

6. M. Henderson *et al.*, "Efficient Natural Language Response Suggestion for Smart Reply", arXiv.org, arXiv:1705.00652, 2017.

7. S. Yavuz *et al.*, "DEEPCOPY: Grounded Response Generation with Hierarchical Pointer Networks", *Proceedings of SIGDial*, 2019.

8. See for example I. Serban *et al.*, "A Deep Reinforcement Learning Chatbot", arXiv.org, arXiv:1709.02349V2, 2017.

9. M. Qui *et al.* "AliMe Chat: A Sequence to Sequence and Rerank Based Chatbot Engine", *Proceedings of the Association for Computational Linguistics*, 2017.

10. L. Zhou *et al.*, "The Design and Implementation of XiaoIce, an Empathetic Social Chatbot", *Computational Linguistics*, 2020.

Chapter 11 – Can You Trust Me?

1. See the smart speaker study report at moniotrlab.ccis.neu.edu/smart-speakers-study.

2. See the Automatic Speaker Verification anti-spoofing website www.asvspoof.org for more information on the various types of spoofing attack and current research attempts to mitigate them.

3. A commonly used technique for generating new data-sets is to use *Wizard-of-Oz* simulation in which a human pretends to be an agent and interacts with a number of paid subjects who have been given specific tasks to perform.

4. See, for example, M. Fredrikson *et al.*, "Model Inversion Attacks That Exploit Confidence Information and Basic Countermeasures", *Proceedings of the ACM Conference on Computer and Communications Security*, 2015.

5. For an explanation of anonymisation in detail see L. García-Sardiña *et al.*, "ES-Port: A Spontaneous Spoken Human–Human Technical Support Corpus for Dialogue Research in Spanish", *Proceedings of the 11th International Conference on Language Resources and Evaluation*, 2018.

6. The European Union's General Data Protection Regulation (GDPR) demands that stored data relating to people must be anonymised. It requires that personal data be rendered anonymous in such a manner that the data subject is not identifiable.

7. M. Abadi *et al.*, "Deep Learning with Differential Privacy", *Proceedings of the 23rd ACM Conference on Computer and Communications Security*, 2016.

8. N. Mehrabi *et al.*, "A Survey on Bias and Fairness in Machine Learning", arXiv.org, arXiv:1908.09635, 2019.

9. S. Sharma *et al.*, "Data Augmentation for Discrimination Prevention and Bias Disambiguation", *Proceedings of the AAAI/ACM Conference on AI, Ethics, and Society*, 2020.

10. J. Kleinberg, S. Mullainathan and M. Raghavan, "Inherent Trade-Offs in the Fair Determination of Risk Scores", arXiv.org, arXiv:1609.05807, 2016.

11. A. Caliskan *et al.*, "Semantics Derived Automatically from Language Corpora Necessarily Contain Human Biases", *Science*, 2017.

12. M. Wolf *et al.*, "Why We Should Have Seen That Coming: Comments on Microsoft's Tay Experiment, and Wider Implications", *ACM Computers and Society*, 2017.

13. E. Aboujaoude *et al.* (Eds), "Digital Interventions in Mental Health: Current Status and Future Directions", *Frontiers in Psychiatry*, 2020.

14. D. Luxton, "Ethical Implications of Conversational Agents in Global Public Health", *Bulletin of the World Health Organisation*, 2020.

15. M. Zhou *et al.*, "Trusting Virtual Agents: The Effect of Personality", *ACM Transactions on Interactive Intelligent Systems*, 2019.

16. T. Hayashi *et al.*, "An Investigation of Multi-speaker Training for Wavenet Vocoder", *IEEE Workshop on Automatic Speech Recognition and Understanding*, 2017.

17. H. Branigan *et al.*, "Linguistic Alignment between People and Computers", *Journal of Pragmatics*, 2020.

Chapter 12 – When All Is Quiet

1. M. Schlichtkrull *et al.*, "Modeling Relational Data with Graph Convolutional Networks", *European Semantic Web Conference*, 2018.

2. See the Trusted Computing Group website trustedcomputinggroup.org.

3. H. McMahan *et al.*, "Communication-Efficient Learning of Deep Networks from Decentralized Data", *International Conference on Artificial Intelligence and Statistics*, 2017.

4. All weight changes submitted by local agents are clipped to a maximum value. This is necessary to ensure that the model training remains within the agreed privacy budget. H. B. McMahan *et al.*, "Learning Differentially Private Recurrent Language Models", *International Conference on Learning Representations*, 2018.

5. Models can be combined by simply interpolating their output distributions.

6. G. Hinton *et al.*, "Distilling the Knowledge in a Neural Network", arXiv.org, arXiv: 1503.02531, 2015.

Chapter 13 – Future Upgrades and Beyond

1. See Y. Leviathan and Y. Matias, "Google Duplex: An AI System for Accomplishing Real-World Tasks Over the Phone", ai.googleblog.com/2018/05/duplex-ai-system-for-natural-conversation.html.

2. R. Levitan *et al.*, "Acoustic–Prosodic Entrainment and Social Behavior", *NAACL Human Language Technology Conference*, 2012.

3. See Tom Gruber's TED talk "How AI Can Enhance Our Memory, Work and Social Lives", at www.ted.com. Tom was a co-inventor of Siri.

4. As an example of a general purpose language model trained using self-supervised learning see J. Devlin *et al.*, "BERT: Pre-training of Deep Bidirectional Transformers for Language Understanding", arXiv.org, arXiv:1810.04805, 2018.

5. For an example of this type of approach to neural reasoning over a knowledge graph see D. A. Hudson and C. D. Manning, "Compositional Attention Networks for Machine Reasoning", *International Conference on Learning Representations*, 2018.

6. These rules are an example of logic programming of which there are many formalisms. Most are derived from Prolog with extensions to improve usability and to guarantee that, unlike in Prolog, a query always terminates. See, for example, V. Lifschitz, *Answer Set Programming*, Springer, 2019.

7. Of course, Paul Simon is an outstanding guitarist but Cyba does not know that.

8. L. de Raedt and A. Kimmig, "Probabilistic Logic Programming Concepts", *Machine Learning*, 2015.

9. Automatically learning rules from stored facts is called *inductive logic programming*, see S. Muggleton and L. de Raedt, "Inductive Logic Programming: Theory and Methods", *Journal of Logic Programming*, 1994.

10. For a related idea, see F. Yang *et al.*, "Differentiable Learning of Logical Rules for Knowledge Base Reasoning", *Conference on Neural Information Processing Systems*, 2017.

11. E. Davis and G. Marcus, "Commonsense Reasoning and Commonsense Knowledge in Artificial Intelligence", *Communications of the ACM*, 2015.

12. Sadly Carrie Fisher passed away in December 2016.

13. R. Kurzweil, *The Singularity Is Near: When Humans Transcend Biology*, Viking, 2005.

14. N. Bostrom, *Superintelligence: Paths, Dangers, Strategies*, Oxford University Press, 2014.

15. See, for example, European Commission, "Ethics Guidelines for Trustworthy AI", ec.europa.eu/futurium/en/ai-alliance-consultation.

Index

Watson, IBM, 5
waveform generation, 123,
    131–134
waveform sample encoding, 132
wavenet, 133
weather domain, 47
web query, 153, 159, 160
    follow-up, 159
web search, 153, 159
web services, 2
web sources, 10
web-based generation, 156
weight, 24, 25, 40, 45, 80, 168,
    179
    count of, 28
    initialisation, 31
    update, 32, 36, 45, 74, 94

weight sharing, 34, 36, 158
Weizenbaum, Joe, 156
Wikidata, 48, 184
Wikipedia, 10
window, 38
Wizard-of-Oz simulation, 99
word, 62, 64, 66, 76
    as translation unit, 144
    boundary of, 67, 145
word embedding, 93–96, 140,
    141, 175
    character-based, 95
worksAt relation, 53, 99

XiaoIce, 6, 164

yes/no questions, 87